Walt Disney
CONVERSATIONS

Conversations with Comic Artists
M. Thomas Inge, General Editor

Walt Disney
CONVERSATIONS

Edited by
Kathy Merlock Jackson

University Press of Mississippi
Jackson

www. upress.state.ms.us

A Mednick Memorial Fellowship aided this work.

This book makes reference to various Disney copyrighted characters, trademarks, marks and registered marks owned by The Walt Disney Company and Disney Enterprises, Inc.

The University Press of Mississippi is a member of the Association of American University Presses.

First edition 2006

∞

Library of Congress Cataloging-in-Publication Data

Disney, Walt, 1901–1966.
  Walt Disney : conversations / edited by Kathy Merlock Jackson.— 1st ed.
     p. cm. — (Conversations with comic artists)
  Includes bibliographical references and index.
    ISBN 1-57806-712-X (alk. paper) — ISBN 1-57806-713-8 (pbk. : alk. paper)
     1. Disney, Walt, 1901–1966. 2. Animators—United States—Interviews.
I. Jackson, Kathy Merlock. II. Title. III. Series.
NC1766.U52D52   2006
791.43'092—dc22   2005047748

British Library Cataloging-in-Publication Data available

Filmography

Walt Disney's Major Entertainment Feature-Length Films

1937	*Snow White and the Seven Dwarfs* (animated)

1937 *Snow White and the Seven Dwarfs* (animated)
1940 *Pinocchio* (animated)
1940 *Fantasia* (animated)
1941 *The Reluctant Dragon* (animated)
1941 *Dumbo* (animated)
1942 *Bambi* (animated)
1943 *Saludos Amigos* (animated with some live action)
1943 *Victory Through Air Power* (combination of animation and live action)
1944 *The Three Caballeros* (combination of animation and live action)
1946 *Make Mine Music* (animated)
1946 *Song of the South* (combination of live action and animation)
1948 *Melody Time* (animated)
1949 *So Dear to My Heart* (combination of animation and live action)
1949 *The Adventures of Ichabod and Mr. Toad* (animated)
1950 *Cinderella* (animated)
1950 *Treasure Island* (live action)
1951 *Alice in Wonderland* (animated)
1952 *The Story of Robin Hood and His Merry Men* (animated)
1953 *Peter Pan* (animated)
1953 *The Living Desert* (True-Life Adventure)
1953 *The Sword and the Rose* (live action)
1954 *Rob Roy—The Highland Rogue* (live action)
1954 *The Vanishing Prairie* (True-Life Adventure)
1954 *20,000 Leagues Under the Sea* (live action)
1955 *Davy Crockett, King of the Wild Frontier* (live action)
1955 *Lady and the Tramp* (animated)
1955 *The Littlest Outlaw* (live action)
1955 *The African Lion* (True-Life Adventure)
1956 *The Great Locomotive Chase* (live action)
1956 *Davy Crockett and the River Pirates* (live action)
1956 *Secrets of Life* (True-Life Adventure)
1956 *Westward Ho the Wagons!* (live action)
1957 *Johnny Tremain* (live action)
1957 *Perri* (True-Life Fantasy)
1957 *Old Yeller* (live action)
1958 *White Wilderness* (True-Life Adventure)
1958 *White Wilderness* (True-Life Adventure)
1958 *The Light in the Forest* (live action)
1958 *Tonka* (live action)
1959 *Sleeping Beauty* (animated)
1959 *The Shaggy Dog* (live action)
1959 *Darby O'Gill and the Little People* (live action)
1959 *Third Man on the Mountain* (live action)

1960	*Toby Tyler or Ten Weeks with the Circus* (live action)
1960	*Kidnapped* (live action)
1960	*Pollyanna* (live action)
1960	*The Sign of Zorro* (live action)
1960	*Jungle Cat* (live action)
1960	*Ten Who Dared* (live action)
1960	*Swiss Family Robinson* (live action)
1961	*One Hundred and One Dalmatians* (animated)
1961	*The Absent-Minded Professor* (live action)
1961	*The Parent Trap* (live action)
1961	*Nikki, Wild Dog of the North* (live action)
1961	*Greyfriars Bobby* (live action)
1961	*Babes in Toyland* (live action)
1962	*Moon Pilot* (live action)
1962	*Bon Voyage* (live action)
1962	*Big Red* (live action)
1962	*Almost Angels* (live action)
1962	*The Legend of Lobo* (live action)
1962	*In Search of the Castaways* (live action)
1963	*Son of Flubber* (live action)
1963	*Miracle of the White Stallions* (live action)
1963	*Savage Sam* (live action)
1963	*Summer Magic* (live action)
1963	*The Incredible Journey* (live action)
1963	*The Three Lives of Thomasina* (live action)
1963	*The Sword and the Stone* (animated)
1964	*The Misadventures of Merlin Jones* (live action)
1964	*A Tiger Walks* (live action)
1964	*The Moon-Spinners* (live action)
1964	*Mary Poppins* (combination of live action with animation)
1964	*Emil and the Detectives* (live action)
1965	*Those Calloways* (live action)
1965	*The Monkey's Uncle* (live action)
1965	*That Darn Cat!* (live action)
1966	*The Ugly Dachshund* (live action)
1966	*Lt. Robin Crusoe U.S.N.* (live action)
1966	*The Fighting Prince of Donegal* (live action)
1966	*Follow Me, Boys!* (live action)
1967	*Monkeys, Go Home!* (live action)*
1967	*The Adventures of Bullwhip Griffin* (live action)*
1967	*The Happiest Millionaire* (live action)*
1967	*The Gnome-Mobile* (live action)*
1967	*The Jungle Book* (animated)*

*Produced by Disney but released after his death

Contents

Introduction

Walt Disney is best remembered for images, not words. In the popular imagination, the Disney name remains synonymous with Mickey Mouse, as well as other memorable animated characters: Snow White, Donald Duck, Pinocchio, Dumbo, Goofy, Bambi, Peter Pan, Uncle Scrooge, Cinderella, Sleeping Beauty. Essentially, though, Walt Disney's real skill lay in his use of words—his interactions and conversations. While only an average artist and writer, he excelled as an oral storyteller, motivator, and persuader. Perhaps the best early example of this occurs in the often-told story of the inception of Disney's first animated feature, *Snow White and the Seven Dwarfs* (1937). Disney gave his animators sixty-five cents each to go across the street and buy dinner at the local beanery. When they returned, he began to tell them the story of Snow White, complete with dramatic voices, sound effects, and songs. As animator Ken Anderson recalled, "We sat there from 8:00 to about 11:30 spellbound" (quoted in Thomas interview). Disney's performance and the subsequent conversation about the production motivated them, and Anderson noted, "We didn't mind, on *Snow White*, working Saturdays and Sundays and nights, which we did. . . . We gave every ounce of everything we had." Years later, animator Frank Thomas added succinctly, "He had a talent to draw out of guys what they didn't have" (quoted in Maltin 29). As Walt Disney's reputation grew, his conversations became pivotal in expressing his vision to both his inner circle and the great mass audience that followed his every move.

This volume collects Disney's conversations about his long and multi-faceted career with journalists and others in the popular media. From the Depression era until Disney's death on 15 December 1966, everyone wanted to talk to, listen to, and read about the famous man behind the mouse. Capturing the sentiment of many journalists, George Kent began his description of a 1938 interview with Disney with the following words: "Of all the glamour-soaked men and women of Hollywood, I was deeply interested in talking to only one—Walt Disney." Nearly a decade later, Frank Nugent of the *New York Times Magazine* appeared at the Disney Studio and announced simply, "I want to interview Mickey."

By the 1940s, Disney was one of the most interviewed people in the world, and cover stories on him appeared in periodicals as diverse as *Barron's, The Miniature Locomotive, Variety, TV Guide, Motion Picture Herald, Look, Time, Newsweek, Ladies' Home Journal*, and the *Saturday Evening Post.* His daily diaries, preserved today at the Walt Disney Archives in Burbank, California, record numerous meetings with print and broadcast journalists throughout the United States and abroad, coinciding with each of his career ventures. Although relatively few interviews with Walt Disney appeared in print in the classic question-answer format, Disney often took the opportunity—in correspondence interviews, radio spots, lectures, and press conferences—to promote his projects, respond to criticisms and concerns, and enhance his public persona.

Disney's public persona, created in interviews, cover stories, and other publicity opportunities, was carefully constructed. Always mindful that his company bore his name and that he was the person most responsible for its image, Disney tried his best to be visible and accessible to his co-workers as well as cooperative with the media. In interview after interview, he related the same rags-to-riches tales about his humble Midwestern beginnings, such as selling newspapers as a child for a few pennies and telling a dentist who wanted him to make a film that he could not come to his office because, he said, "I haven't any shoes. . . . They were falling apart and I left them at the shoemaker's. He won't let me have them until I can dig up a dollar and a half" (Miller, "My Dad," 130; Molloy interview). He told Tony Thomas in a recorded interview in January 1959: "I came to Hollywood . . . in August 1923, with $30 in my pocket and . . . a coat and pair of trousers that didn't match. And one half of my suitcase had my shirts and underwear and things—the other half had my drawing materials. . . . It was a cardboard suitcase at that."

Although Disney's interviewers were quick to emphasize his wealth, they were equally ready to downplay its importance to his lifestyle, observing Disney's preference for casual, even shabby dress and his disdain for Hollywood society in preference to spending time at home with his family or tinkering with his miniature railroad (Miller, "Suddenly" 100). "I think of money as a tool," Disney remarked in a 1956 article in the *Saturday Evening Post*. "I don't want to bank dividends from my Disney stock. I'd rather keep the money working" (Miller, "Disney's Folly"). His assessment remained steadfast by 1962 when he observed in a 1962 *Newsweek* interview that "[d]ollars, like fertilizer, make things grow." He often retorted, as he did in a 1956 interview with Edith Efron of *TV Guide*, that "[m]oney doesn't excite me—my ideas excite me" (12). Collectively, Disney's interviews suggest that he never rejected his humble beginnings. He affirmed to Frank Rasky of the Toronto *Star Weekly* in a 1964 interview that "you'll not find a single mousetrap around the house. I've never forgotten it was a mouse that made me what I am today."

Comments on that persona extended beyond mere talk. One of the most popular interviews with Disney, an eight-part series that ran in the *Saturday Evening Post* in late 1956 and early 1957, was featured under the byline of his daughter Diane Disney Miller as told to Martin. These varied articles, resulting from an interviewer's time spent with Disney often on the studio lot or at Disneyland, reveal not only what Disney said but also the enthusiastic tone of his voice, his raspy smoker's cough, his casual clothes and pockets filled with crunchy snacks, and the flurry of activity that surrounded him on a given day.

Part of the public's fascination with the Disney persona stemmed from the circumstances of his success. His rise to popularity and wealth coincided roughly with the middle years of the twentieth century, and his words, popularized by the print and broadcast media, speak not only to his own professional development but also to larger cultural issues at play in America. By the 1950s, when Disney achieved the pinnacle of his popularity, America had endured the Great Depression, World War II, and the Korean War, and had emerged a richer country than it had ever been previously. Craving normalcy and upward mobility, Americans married in record numbers, setting the stage for the greatest baby boom the world has ever known. Between 1946 and 1964, 76 million babies were born, the peak occurring in 1957 (Jones 2). Hoping for greater opportunities, many veterans took advantage of the G.I. Bill, pursuing college educations that they believed would lead to comfortable houses in the suburbs and better, more affluent lives for themselves and their families. They also embraced new technologies, especially television and state-of-the-art automobiles, as America became a rapidly modernized culture.

Disney seemed to be the personification of this American moment and the American Dream. He had built enormous wealth and a multinational creative enterprise from scratch, but projected an aura of being down-to-earth and humble. He embraced advanced technology and ideas but paradoxically used them to create nostalgic visions of the past. (Tellingly, many of his most popular film productions—among them, *Sleeping Beauty, Snow White and the Seven Dwarfs, Old Yeller, Davy Crockett*, and *Pinocchio*—are set in the distant past or based on old fairy tales.)

Disney's dedication to work as a moral good also mirrored that of the Protestant work ethic so central to American culture. He often noted that, as a young man, he toiled in a post office "twelve or fourteen hours a day, I thought it was a gold rush" (Miller, "Hard Times," 75). The habit stuck. In a 1957 profile in *Time* magazine titled "Father Goose," Disney asserted that he worked fourteen hours a day and never took a vacation. "I get enough vacation," he said, "from getting a change of troubles" (43).

The result of his hard work was the success sought by so many upwardly mobile Americans. Financially, Disney related to journalists how far he had come. In a 1955 interview with Arthur Gordon for a cover story in *Look* magazine, he noted how when his brother and financial advisor Roy Disney told him that they owed several million dollars, Walt started to laugh. When Roy asked what was so funny, Disney responded, "I was just remembering . . . the days when we couldn't afford to owe even a thousand dollars because no one would lend us that much!" (Gordon 4). Four years later, in an interview with Lee Edson for *Think* magazine, Disney reflected on Disneyland, noting that "five years ago Disneyland was just a flat plain of orange groves. It cost us $4,500 an acre. The bank recently appraised it. Know for how much? $20,000 an acre. Imagine, $20,000 an acre." After recounting this information, Edson writes, "Disney paused—a bit awed, I thought, by his own swift success."

That success, however, also displayed a crucial conflict in Disney's life and philosophy. Like America itself, he was torn between two ideals: the drive to advance materially and technologically and the desire to stay connected to the simplicities of the past, family, and nature.

On one hand, Disney espoused to his interviewers his attraction to television, animatronics, and futuristic projects, such as the live-action adaptation of Jules Verne's novel *20,000 Leagues Under the Sea*. In an interview published in *TV Guide* in 1957, he observed, "The age we're living in is the most extraordinary the world has ever seen. There are new concepts of things, and we now have the tools to change those concepts into realities. We are moving forward" ("Extraordinary" 19). While other filmmakers rejected television, seeing it as dangerous competition, Disney saw its potential and embraced it, becoming one of the first movie studio heads to begin creating programming for the small screen. "I'm really having fun with television," Disney enthused in an interview. "I haven't had so much fun since my early days in the business when I had the latitude to experiment. With TV, it's like a cage has been opened—and I can fly again" ("Extraordinary" 19). He was equally excited about a new technology—animatronics—proclaiming at a Florida press conference announcing plans for a new theme park, that "it's all electronically controlled. It's another dimension in our world of animating that inanimate . . . and with that it's a new door" ("Florida Press Conference" 10).

Yet Walt Disney was just as connected to the past, peppering his 1950s movie releases with frontier stories like *Davy Crockett* and *Old Yeller* and folktale adaptations such as *Song of the South*. He fashioned Disneyland as a place steeped in an idealized past that existed more in his mind than in reality. The houses on Main Street, for example, are 80 percent smaller than normal, and all else, including the horses that pull the carriages, are miniature versions, designed to be more easily grasped (Gordon 29).

Disney symbolized a cultural tension of America's industrial society: the future as represented by technology versus the past as represented by nostalgia. According to Disney's daily diaries, he had an interview with *Look* magazine's Arthur Gordon scheduled for March 4, 1955, and on April 2 took him to preview Disneyland, which would open in July. Gordon's cover story ran on July 26, 1955, with the following opening statement: "Disneyland is not only a living monument to a living man; it is a surprisingly accurate map of the complicated mass of little gray cells that make up the mind of Walt Disney. All the apparent paradoxes are there: Nostalgia jammed up against needle-point promises of the future" (Gordon 29).

In his attempt to recreate the past, Disney exhibited strong patriot-ism, once remarking, "I get red, white, and blue, all over" (*Walt* 40). In an interview with Lee Edson at *Think* magazine, Disney commented on a Disneyland feature called the Pageant of Presidents. "It's the story of America through the Presidents. . . . I'll have Lincoln standing up and delivering an address." His intense Americanism proved especially in sync with the nation during the World War II years but raised suspicion when he was reported to be an F.B.I. informant during the Red Scare. He testified before the House Un-American Activities Committee (HUAC) in 1947, naming names and asserting his patriotism.

Disney tapped into another cultural conflict that came to the fore-front in the 1950s and 1960s: suburbanization and planned communities versus untouched nature. The Levittown experiment, which provided the first mass-produced suburban communities, placed the building of planned communities on the public agenda. Thus, Disneyland, with its state-of-the-art architecture, landscaping, and transportation, was in sync with Americans' priorities. Telling interviewer Lee Edson about his proposed theme park, Disney explained excitedly, "We're going to have a monorail . . . like the one in Cologne, Germany. . . . You know, I think monorail is going to be the rapid transit of the future, and we'll be giving a preview of it."

In contrast to suburban planning, however, Disney's priorities equated with nature. By the 1950s, although the back-to-nature movement of the 1960s movement was still a decade away, the easy accessibility of automobiles led to a trend in autocamping as many Americans drove off to visit nature. Disney's new series of nature documentaries, called the True-Life Adventures, did remarkably well and generated much press coverage. They include titles such as *Seal Island, Beaver Valley, Nature's Half Acre, The Olympic Elk, Water Birds,* and *The Living Desert.* In a 1953 interview for *Newsweek* magazine, Disney likened his nature stories to animation and explained their attraction to audiences. "In making any comparisons between real and animation animals," he declared, "it must be borne in mind that the cartoon critters—that is, figures of fable—have always been a combination of human and animal appearance and traits. . . . And animals behaving like humans are univer-sally considered as very amusing. Similarly, wild or domestic animals are funny when they most closely ape human behavior in their romantic antics, their angers and anxieties, their greed and stupidities" ("Peter Pan" 98).

Even his explanation of his work was often discussed in natural terms. Disney told similar versions of the following tale to several magazines:

> You know, I was stumped one day when a little boy asked, "Do you draw Mickey Mouse?" I had to admit I didn't draw anymore. "Then you think up all the jokes and ideas?" "No," I said, "I don't do that." Finally, he looked at me and said: "Mr. Disney, just what do you do?" . . . "Well," I said, "sometimes I think of myself as a little bee. I go from one area of the studio to another and gather pollen and sort of stimulate everybody. I guess that's the job I do." (Bright 303)

A final way in which Disney reflected his culture's preoccupations regards his connection with children during the Baby Boom. He built Disneyland, he said, to recapture the joy that he had when he took his two daughters to the zoo or amusement park when they were young. His movies, which he always claimed "are for everyone!" ("Valuator" 13), especially appealed to children, whom he regarded with respect and never talked down to. As Disney told Don Eddy of *New American Magazine* in a 1955 interview,

> I don't believe in playing down to children. I don't treat my youngsters like fragile flowers, and I think no parent should. Children are people and they should have to reach and learn about things, to understand things, just as adults have to reach if they want to grow in mental stature. Life is composed of lights and shadows, and we would be untruthful, insincere, and sacharine if we tried to pretend there were no shadows. . . . You do a child no favor by trying to shield it from reality.

And herein lies another conflict. While some said Disney catered to children, others criticized him for being too graphic, such as in a True-Life Adventure that showed the birth of a buffalo calf. Disney refused to cut the scene and said, "Aren't we getting prudish . . . when we say natural processes are objectionable? I want my children to know about these things, and to learn them from nature; they are part of existence, as natural and unashamed as breathing."

Disney took pains to come across as a man as natural and casual as a breath of fresh air. Variants of the stories above were related by Disney as well as promoted by his family, friends, and staff. He was determined to make interviews work for him to promote his projects, just as he realized that media outlets were using him to promote and sell themselves.

Journalists, of course, had their own agendas as well. To a large extent, journalists bring their own and their culture's predispositions to an interview. Dustin Hoffman once recounted his own experience with an interviewer: "I had just Beacon-waxed my floor and she came in, smelled, and says, 'You been smoking pot in here?' And I said, 'That's Beacon wax.' And she says, 'Come on . . . I know what you people do'" (quoted in Silvester 2). To this Hoffman lamented, "They've already decided what you are" (2). Perhaps, too, in the case of Walt Disney, they had already decided what he was. It is important to note that while a public figure and his or her press secretary determine accessibility for an interview and its parameters, in a typical face-to-face interview situation, the journalist has control, asking the questions while the subject answers. The journalist determines the topic and direction of the interview: what questions are asked in what order, and how intently. Further, both parties understand that the results of the interview—shaped, interpreted, edited, and prioritized—will be made public (Silvester 42). Collectively interviews paint a portrait of a public figure. They also reflect the sensibilities of individual journalists and the society they represent.

To control how he was presented and shaped by the media insofar as it was possible, Disney employed a publicist named Joe Reddy who, for many years, became effectively the voice of Disney. Reddy ferreted out the many requests for interviews with Disney, coordinating access to the busy executive, and worked diligently with journalists publishing interviews and profiles. He oversaw many interviews with Disney that were conducted in writing.

One such interview has an interesting history. David Griffiths of the *TV Times of London*, which had the largest circulation of any commercial television journal in England, attempted to interview Disney in his hotel while he was in London negotiating the sale of a television series. Unfortunately, Disney was about to leave the country but invited Griffiths to send his questions to the Burbank Studio. Disney approved responses to the questions on March 10, 1959, and the reply was sent to Griffiths. However, the deal never materialized, and Griffiths never wrote the article—until he found his notes in the bottom of a drawer two decades later years. Eventually, the results of Griffiths's interview with Disney were published in *Popular Video* in August 1981, coinciding with the release of new Disney videos in England.

The articles presented here are arranged chronologically in the order in which the conversations with Disney occurred and are not edited for duplication of material or contradiction, so as to preserve the essence of what Disney said. This organization best demonstrates the development of key themes that dominated Disney's life.

Interviews provide only a glimpse into the life of a public figure. They may tell much more about the people who write and consume them: what they care about and what they want to hear. In the case of Walt Disney's conversations, one thing is certain: Disney understood the cultural milieu and played to it, representing in many cases opposite sides of a key issue. He expressed Americans' reach for success, as well as their nostalgia for the past, labors in the present, and excitement for the future. As such, it is fitting that we scrutinize not only the cinematic images that Disney oversaw but also the words that he spoke.

This book began with a suggestion from Tom Inge, a kind and generous scholar who has always been one of my greatest inspirations. As Tom told me about Conversations with Comic Artists, a new series of books he was editing for the University Press of Mississippi, he reminded me a bit of Walt Disney, whose unbridled enthusiasm for a project was infectious. By the time I saw the first book in the series, Tom's on Charles M. Schulz, I was committed. I knew I wanted to play a part in the series and appreciate Tom's invitation to do so. Editor Seetha Srinivasan followed up with a contract and the type of literary support that can only come from a professionally run publishing house; she and the University Press of Mississippi are first rate.

Having secured the University Press of Mississippi contract, I began trying to secure funding to travel to the Walt Disney Archives in Burbank, California, to do research. The Mednick Foundation of Virginia responded with a generous grant, for which I will always be grateful. I also received support, as a Batten Scholar, from the Frank and Jane Batten Fund, and I cherish being a member of the many professors who benefited from the Battens' academic philanthropy. At the Disney Archives, I encountered a staff of helpful accomplices in my search to learn more about Disney. Archivist Dave Smith knows more about Walt Disney than anyone else alive, and I appreciate his advice in helping me to find the precise sources I was seeking. His staff members, including Robert Tieman, Becky Cline, Collette Espino, and Adina Lerner, provided not only bibliographic support but also good cheer and much anecdotal information about Disney which allowed me to better understand the man and the studio that he founded. Although I had been at the Disney Archives a decade earlier when researching another book, this time the place was much busier, an indication of how much the organization had grown. I know that Margaret Adamic, who must approve researchers' admittance into the archives, did not have to let me in since the facility is no longer open to those outside the company, but I'm appreciative that she did. It has made all the difference in this book. I also thank the Walt Disney Company for giving me permission to reprint archival material and images. Working with these professionals has been a pleasure.

Back home in Virginia, I found a campus environment that promoted my research. I appreciate the continued support of my college president, William T. Greer, Jr., and academic dean, Stephen S. Mansfield. Two students from Virginia Wesleyan College, Eileen Dubuss and Kelli C. Pippin, conducted Disney research for a January term independent study project. Their zeal in collecting Disney's interviews showed me that others might be eager to read them too. Librarians Mary Carol Lynch, Velma Haley, and Jan Pace got involved, spending endless hours tracking down sources for interlibrary loan and permissions information, while Jesse Fanshaw, with his encyclopedic knowledge of early radio, located audio cassettes capturing some of Disney's most important broadcast interviews.

I also thank Virginia Wesleyan College faculty secretary Barbara Hodges who oversaw the lengthy correspondence process of securing permissions for the various articles that appear here. She cared about this book and was a delight to work with.

Finally, this book would never have reached completion if it were not for the scholarly soul mates who talked with me about it as it traversed its various stages, sharing their ideas and listening to mine. They include my professional colleagues—Bill Jones, Bill Ruehlmann, Eve Blachman, Linda Ferguson, Gary Edgerton, Mike Marsden, and Jack Nachbar—and especially my brother, Ray Merlock, of the University of South Carolina Upstate.

My husband, Joe Jackson, and my son, Nick Jackson, always lavish me not only with their insights but also with their love and laughter; nothing is more important. To them, this book is dedicated.

KMJ

Works Cited

Bright, John. "Disney's Fantasy Empire." *The Nation*, 6 March 1967, 299–303.

Efron, Edith. "Still Attacking His Ancient Enemy—Conformity." *TV Guide*, 17 July 1965, 10–14.

"Father Goose." *Time*, 27 December 1954, 42–46.

Gordon, Arthur. "Walt Disney." *Look*, 26 July 1955, 29–35.

Jones, Landon Y. *Great Expectations: America and the Baby Boom Generation*. New York: Ballantine, 1980.

Maltin, Leonard. *Of Mice and Magic: A History of American Animated Cartoons* (1980). Revised ed. New York: New American Library, 1987.

Miller, Diane Disney (as told to Pete Martin). "Disney's Folly." *Saturday Evening Post*, 22 December 1956, 23–24+.

———. "Hard Times in Kansas City." *Saturday Evening Post*, 24 November 1956, 25–27+.

———. "My Dad, Walt Disney." *Saturday Evening Post*, 17 November 1956, 25–26+.

———. "Suddenly He Was a Genius." *Saturday Evening Post*, 15 December 1956, 36–37+.

"Peter Pan: Real Disney Magic; Real Animals Also Make Money." *Newsweek*, 16 February 1953, 96–99.

Silvester, Christopher, ed. *The Norton Book of Interviews*. New York: Norton, 1993.

"The Valuator Interviews: Walt Disney." *The Valuator*, Summer 1966, 11–13.

Walt. Collection of Walt Disney's quotes, available at the Walt Disney Archives in Burbank, California.

"Wide World of Disney, The." *Newsweek*, 31 December 1962, 18, 49, 50.

Chronology

1901   Walt Disney, the fourth of five children of Elias and Flora
            Call Disney, is born in Chicago on December 5 and named
            after the Congregational minister who baptizes him and his
            father. Father is trained as a carpenter, although he embarks
            on several unrelated business ventures, and mother is a
            former schoolteacher. In childhood, Walt forms a close
            relationship with older brother Roy.

1906   Family moves to Marceline, Missouri, hoping for a more
            wholesome country life, and young Walt develops interests
            in nature and drawing.

1910   Family forced to sell farm for financial reasons and moves to
            Kansas City, Missouri, where Elias becomes a newspaper route
            manager, and brothers Walt and Roy deliver newspapers.

1915   Takes his first professional art lessons at the Kansas City Art
            Institute.

1917   Family moves to Chicago, where Elias assumes part
            ownership of a jelly factory.

1918   Leaves McKinley High School without graduating and,
            although under age, joins the Red Cross Ambulance Corps
            as a driver and serves in France during World War I.

1919   Completes his tour of duty and returns to Kansas City, where brother Roy is a banker. Works as an apprentice for Pesmen-Rubin Commercial Artists. Befriends another talented artist, Ub Iwerks, and they start their own business, Iwerks-Disney Commercial Artists, which lasts only a month.

1920   Hired as an artist at the Kansas City Slide Company (later called the Kansas City Film Ad Company), where Ub Iwerks eventually joins him, and they learn the basics of animation.

1922   Opens garage studio and produces a series of films for the Newman Theater Company called Newman Laugh-O-Grams. Leaves his job at Kansas City Film Ad, incorporates Laugh-O-Gram Films, and convinces Ub Iwerks to join him.

1923   Moves to Hollywood after company goes bankrupt and lives with his Uncle Robert. Starts the Walt Disney Company with the help of his brother Roy and, later, Ub Iwerks. Lands first contract, with distributor M. J. Winkler, to produce a series called the Alice Comedies, conceived while in Kansas City.

1924   Experiments with a technique combining live-action and animation and releases *Alice's Day at Sea*, the first of his Alice's Comedies series, for M. J. Winkler. Moves into a small store at 4649 Kingswell that has an adjoining garage for his office.

1925   On July 13, marries Lillian Bounds of Lewiston, Idaho, who works for his company as an inker and painter. Earlier that year, on April 17, Roy Disney marries Edna Francis, and Walt serves as his best man.

1926   Walt Disney Studio moves to a new facility at 2719 Hyperion Avenue.

1927   Releases the first Oswald the Lucky Rabbit cartoon but loses the popular character to Universal, which owns full rights. Conceives a new character, a mouse named Mickey.

1928   Releases *Steamboat Willie*, the first animated film with synchronized sound and the first to feature Mickey Mouse, for whom he provides a distinctive falsetto voice, and Minnie

Mouse. Film opens at the Colony Theater in New York on November 18 and is an instant success.

1929   Releases *Skeleton Dance*, the first film in the Silly Symphony series, with an eerie tone and highly developed synchronized movement that are ground-breaking for the time.

1930   Oversees the inception of the first Mickey Mouse comic strip.

1931   Suffers a nervous breakdown due to exhaustion from overwork and takes a vacation to recuperate. Mickey Mouse becomes a worldwide phenomenon, and the Mickey Mouse Club reaches a million members.

1932   Releases the Silly Symphony *Flowers and Trees*, the first full-color cartoon and the first to win an Academy Award; also wins a special Academy Award for the creation of Mickey Mouse. Forms an art school at the studio to train animators and perfects the use of the storyboard. Signs a contract with Herman (Kay) Kamen for the merchandising of high-quality Disney character-themed products, including two of the most successful items, Lionel trains and Ingersoll-Waterbury watches.

1933   Daughter Diane Marie born on December 18. Releases *Three Little Pigs*, the second Silly Symphony to win an Academy Award. Film's optimistic message regarding the ability to overcome adversity strikes a chord with Depression audiences, and theme song "Who's Afraid of the Big Bad Wolf?" becomes a hit.

1934   Introduces Donald Duck in the Silly Symphony *The Wise Little Hen*.

1935   Releases *The Band Concert*, the first Mickey Mouse cartoon in color.

1936   Second daughter, Sharon Mae, born on January 1. Brother Roy, fearing that Disney is exhausted and heading for another nervous breakdown, suggests a ten-year anniversary trip to Europe for the two of them and their wives. Receives a special award in Paris from the French Legion of

Honor for "creating an art form in which good is spread throughout the world" and is convinced of the international appeal of his films.

1937 Releases *The Old Mill*, the first animated short to use the multiplane camera. Wins an Academy Award for the film and a special Academy Award for the multiplane camera, which provides visual depth in animation by shooting through layers of film. Releases *Snow White and the Seven Dwarfs*, the first feature-length animated film, which premieres on December 21 at the Carthay Circle Theater in Los Angeles and goes on to win a special Academy Award.

1938 Releases the animated short *Ferdinand the Bull*, which wins an Academy Award. Mother Flora Disney dies of asphyxiation due to a faulty furnace in a house that Disney and brother Roy had recently purchased for their parents.

1940 Releases two feature-length animated films, *Pinocchio* and *Fantasia*, and moves operation to a spacious new studio in Burbank, California.

1941 Oversees an unauthorized strike of the Screen Cartoonists Guild at his studio. Releases *The Reluctant Dragon* and *Dumbo* and travels to South America on a goodwill trip. Father Elias Disney dies. U.S. Army moves onto the Disney Studio lot immediately following the bombing of Pearl Harbor.

1942 Releases *Bambi*, distinctive for its animated realism.

1943 Releases *Der Fuehrer's Face*, an Academy-Award winning animated short starring Donald Duck; *Saludos Amigos* promoting a "good neighbor" policy toward Latin America; and *Victory through Air Power*.

1945 Releases *The Three Caballeros*, an animated and live-action release to further establish a "good neighbor" policy toward Latin America.

1946 Releases *Make Mine Music* and *Song of the South*.

1947 Releases *Fun and Fancy Free*. Travels to Alaska with his daughter Sharon, a trip inspired by Alfred and Emma

Millotte's documentary footage for what would become
Seal Island.

1948   Releases *Melody Time* and *Seal Island*, the first True-Life
Adventure, which wins an Academy Award for Best Short
Subject.

1949   Releases *So Dear to My Heart* and *The Adventures of
Ichabod and Mr. Toad*. Establishes the Walt Disney Music
Company. Takes one of many trips to England with his family.

1950   Releases *Cinderella* and the studio's first completely live-
action feature, *Treasure Island*. Airs his first television show,
a Christmas Day special titled *One Hour in Wonderland*.

1951   Releases *Alice in Wonderland*.

1952   Releases *The Story of Robin Hood*. Establishes WED
Enterprises.

1953   Releases *Peter Pan*; the first People and Places documentary
The Alaskan Eskimo; The Sword and the Rose; and the
True-Life Adventure *The Living Desert*, which wins an
Academy Award for best documentary feature.

1954   Releases *Rob Roy, the Highland Rogue, The Vanishing
Prairie*, and *20,000 Leagues Under the Sea*. Begins airing his
first television series, *The Wonderful World of Disney*,
which features a popular episode on Davy Crockett.
Daughter Diane marries Ron Miller on May 9.

1955   Releases *Davy Crockett, King of the Wild Frontier; Lady and
the Tramp; The African Lion*; and *The Littlest Outlaw*.
Oversees the opening of new theme park, Disneyland, in
Anaheim, California, on July 17. Airs the first *Mickey Mouse
Club* show on television. First grandchild, Christopher
Disney Miller, is born in spring.

1956   Releases *The Great Locomotive Chase, Davy Crockett and
the River Pirates, Secrets of Life*, and *Westward Ho the
Wagons!* Daughter Diane Disney Miller's eight-part series,
"My Dad, Walt Disney," begins running in the *Saturday
Evening Post*.

1957   Releases *Johnny Tremain, Perri,* and *Old Yeller.* Airs the first
            episode of *Zorro* on television.

1958   Releases *The Light in the Forest, Wild Wilderness,* and *Tonka.*

1959   Releases *Sleeping Beauty, The Shaggy Dog, Darby O'Gill
            and the Little People,* and *Third Man on the Mountain.
            Sleeping Beauty,* expected to be a masterpiece, is critical and
            popular disappointment, and studio, while not abandoning
            expensive animated projects, begins to concentrate on low-
            budget, profitable, live-action fare. Daughter Sharon marries
            Bob Brown on May 10. Leaves in June for England, the first
            of four trips he will make there over the next two years.

1960   Releases *Toby Tyler, or Ten Weeks with the Circus;
            Kidnapped; Pollyanna; The Sign of Zorro; Jungle Cat; Ten
            Who Dared;* and *Swiss Family Robinson.*

1961   Releases *One Hundred and One Dalmatians; The Absent-
            Minded Professor; The Parent Trap; Nikki, Wild Dog of the
            North; Greyfriars Bobby,* and *Babes in Toyland.* Establishes
            the California Institute of the Arts. Grandson and namesake
            Walter Elias Disney Miller is born on November 14.

1962   Releases *Moon Pilot, Bon Voyage!, Big Red, Almost Angels,
            The Legend of Lobo,* and *In Search of the Castaways.*

1963   Releases *Son of Flubber, Miracle of the White Stallions,
            Savage Sam, Summer Magic, The Incredible Journey,* and
            The Sword in the Stone. Introduces Audio-Animatronics in
            the Enchanted Tiki Room attraction at Disneyland. Selects
            central Florida as the site of his next theme park.

1964   Releases *The Misadventures of Merlin Jones, A Tiger Walks,
            The Three Lives of Thomasina, The Moon-Spinners, Emil
            and the Detectives,* and *Mary Poppins,* his greatest cine-
            matic success since *Snow White and the Seven Dwarfs.*
            Opens four exhibits at the New York World's Fair. Accepts
            the Presidential Medal for Freedom from President Lyndon
            Johnson on September 14.

1965   Releases *Those Calloways, The Monkey's Uncle,* and
            That Darn Cat! Purchases land in central Florida for his
            Experimental Prototype City of Tomorrow (EPCOT) and an
            East Coast version of his Disneyland theme park.

1966   Releases *The Ugly Dachshund; Lt. Robin Crusoe, U.S.N.; The Fighting Prince of Donegal*; and *Follow Me, Boys!* Establishes a design for EPCOT as high-technology, functioning community and travels throughout the United States to inspect cities in order to generate new ideas for EPCOT. Takes a thirteen-day yacht cruise with his wife, daughters, and their families in the waters off the coast of British Columbia. Is diagnosed with cancer and undergoes surgery for the removal of his left lung in November. Dies on December 15 of lung cancer at the age of sixty-five. Survived by his wife of forty-one years, two daughters, and seven grandchildren.

1967   Studio releases *Monkeys, Go Home!; The Adventures of Bullwhip Griffin; The Happiest Millionaire; The Gnome-Mobile; The Jungle Book*; and *Charlie the Lonesome Cougar*, the last films Disney personally produced.

Walt Disney
CONVERSATIONS

How Silly Symphonies and Mickey Mouse Hit the Up Grade

FLORABEL MUIR / 1929

From *New York Sunday News*,
December 1, 1929, n.p.

A crew of cartoonists and an orchestra working under the supervision of
Walt Disney turn out the work while Walt looks out to see that the bills
are paid and enough money rolls in to meet the payroll.

"Who's the president or head of this concern?" I asked.

"We haven't any president or any other officers," Walt explained.
"In fact, we are not even incorporated. I guess you couldn't call us a company. We just get together the bunch of us, and work things out. We voice
our opinions and sometimes we have good old-fashioned scraps but in the
end things get ironed out and we have something we're all proud of."

Walt began his career in Chicago where he went to art school. When
he was about seventeen he picked up odd jobs on the Chicago *Tribune*
working on layouts, and from there he drifted to Kansas City and tried to
peddle his talents to the Kansas City *Star*.

"But I guess fate was against letting me be a successful cartoonist," he told me. "Gosh, how I used to envy the guys who were knocking out what looked like big jack in those days and I wondered if I could ever reach the top. I finally turned my eyes to Hollywood, where I decided I would go and try to become a director."

. . .

"It is the rhythm that has appealed to the public," Walt told me. "The action flows along and we have to work hard to keep the movement flowing with the music. We had to work it out mathematically."

"We try to get something in the cartoon besides just nonsense. Some ideas such as in the Silly Symphony where the idea of thousands of members of the animal kingdom preying on each other was carried out. We have to be careful not to get the sketches too silly."

. . .

"Don't ask me if we're making money," Walt begged. "I wouldn't know about that. I know we're getting by all right. My brother turns up here each week with enough to pay everybody off. We haven't found time yet to sit around and count our profits."

"Everybody here has his shoulders to the wheel," Walt said. "Maybe sometime we'll all be rolling in wealth and move into more pretentious quarters and put on the high hat, but we won't be making any better movies."

Snow White's Daddy

GEORGE KENT / 1938

From *The Family Circle*, vol. 12, no. 25,
June 24, 1938, pp. 10–11, 16.

Of all the glamour-soaked men and women of Hollywood, I was
deeply interested in talking to only one—Walt Disney. He owns his
company, he take orders from nobody, and he has never tried to put
out anything short of the best. And as far as I was concerned, he was
and still is one of the film colony's most thoroughly sincere and
honest men.

Therefore, exactly eighty minutes after I alighted from the train in
Los Angeles I got into a taxi and told the driver to take me posthaste to
the Disney studios. Unlike other studios, there were no men in cowboy
suits, no members of the Foreign Legion, no British grenadiers stalking
about.

"Yes, Mr. Disney will see you," said the girl at the switchboard, "but
he's tied up for several hours. Would you like to spend the time looking

around and seeing how the cartoons are made?" Would I? Can Donald Duck fight?

In a few minutes a guide popped through the door. He was a little man with a crinkled, good-humored face whom the people around the studio, he told me, call Ducky. He explained that he is Donald's voice. I looked at this gentle soul and sniffed skeptically. So he showed me.

Right there in a corridor he burst into a violent, half-berserk quackery, filled with "Wassamatter—wanna fight? Gwan! Startin' somethin'? Honk! Quack!" I was convinced.

Ducky does other animals, too, but Donald's voice is his life work—that and showing visitors through the studio. Before joining Disney, Ducky had worn the uniform of a milk company and had gone from school to school entertaining kids with his imitations. The milk company paid him $35 a week. Then somehow he got on the air and Walt heard him. Now he earns $200 weekly. (The Disney studio is full of such stories.)

At our first stop on the studio tour I learned something about the cartoon business which I had never suspected goes on. Ducky took me into a room where three coatless men were sitting in wicker chairs look-ing intently at the movie of a cow—not Clarabelle or any other cartoon figure but just a cow. And it wasn't my idea of a red-hot film. First it showed a calf eating grass. Then the calf grew up and ate more grass. Finally—as the big, smashing climax—she gave a few gallons of milk! The end.

Ho-hum, thought I. Yet there sat three men, who I assumed were clever, chirping excited comments. I looked again at the picture. Was I missing something, or was it true that there's a germ in the air of Hollywood which turns sensible people into crackpots?

"Look!" suddenly cried a curly-headed member of the trio, who could easily have passed for a professor of physics. "No matter how fat a cow gets, her hips still stay bony."

"And look!" he piped a moment later. "Watch that line that moves along her nose when she eats!"

"Uh-huh," grunted a bald-headed companion. "And when she eats, she moves her jaws from side to side instead of up and down the way we do."

I chewed silently to myself. By cracky—the man was right! Cows *do* chew from side to side.

Then I found out that these three men were artists—three of the more than 250 artists who draw pictures of animals for the Disney cartoons. This cow was their model, demonstrating to them how a cow walks, eats, runs, and lies down. Which is important in the animated cartoon business because these artists do not draw pictures to hang in frames. Instead, they make drawings of beasts and birds and people which when put together will give the subject the appearance of moving like the real thing. It's a specialized branch of art, one which demands that the artist have a knowledge of anatomy in motion. So few persons are able to do a good job of this kind of drawing that Walt has been obliged to set up a training school in which the elements of animation are taught to talented young men.

The three men I saw had been sitting in those same chairs for three days, studying their cow model. And when they had finished talking over what they had seen and had sketched the model numerous times, they knew they could put her on celluloid and make her do everything a cow can do, and even what a cow hadn't oughter ever do, whenever they wanted to. Later, they would supplement their knowledge by going to nearby farms to watch a live model.

What finally goes on the film is, however, no slavish imitation of a live animal, for the true to life sketch which looks all right on the wall simply will not do when worked into action.

Take, for example, deer like the ones in *Snow White* and in *Little Hiawatha*. Ducky introduced me to the artist who made the deer drawings, and that young man explained that when he first animated a deer, he was dissatisfied. And so was everybody else. The trouble, he said, was that the deer just didn't seem to run very fast, which was all wrong because a deer can usually outrun a horse, yet horses in the cartoons, when drawn faithfully, seemed to be going at a terrific speed. The artist thought about the problem and finally decided that the deer seemed slow because it ran too smoothly. So into the move-ment of the deer he grafted the galloping motion of a horse. And it did the trick.

When Disney's artists were studying pigs, they discovered that in a healthy porker the tail is tightly coiled, and that in a weak one there's no curl at all. This little tidbit of information came in handy when work started on *Three Little Pigs*. Do you remember how the tails coiled and uncoiled and how it gave the animals added vitality? In real life, of course, pigs don't behave that way at all, but it was an exaggeration which definitely helped. Without study, this delightful and characteristic Disney touch would not have been thought of.

When *Three Little Pigs* was first started, the studio considered putting the pigs on four feet, but, as one artist explained it, that way a hog is like a tank, and you can't do much with it. So they reared them up on their hind legs—and with results which we all remember gratefully.

Sheep also gave the artists trouble. When they sketched them as they are, the ripply line down their back to show their wooliness looked great on the drawing board, but in action it gave the impression of water. Keep your eyes open for the next cartoon sheep and you will see that the wool is represented by an almost straight line.

Often study suggests gags, as it did in the case of a horse. When a horse runs, the artists observed, its neck goes down level with the body, and the tail out behind. It occurred to one of the staff, as he looked at the drawings, that if you pushed on the tail, the running horse's head, which was on a straight line with the tail, could be made to move forward. This idea was used in a film of a horse race, with the jockey seizing the tail and shoving the head forward to win the grand steeplechase in a photo finish.

Remember the rabbit in *The Tortoise and the Hare*? The hare was so quick on his feet that he was able to play tennis with himself and, in baseball, dash to the plate and bat the ball which he himself had thrown from the pitcher's box. Well, that rabbit was half wallaby. A friend had presented Walt with a pair of them and for a long time they were the studio pets. From watching their antics, the artists got the idea for the lightning-speed rabbit which we saw in the cartoon.

Donald Duck, as you probably have noticed, waddles inordinately, moving with a sort of ferryboat motion. He does that because the artists had trouble distinguishing between a duck and a goose, on paper, and decided to exaggerate Donald's walk.

Roosters in a Silly Symphony stretch abnormally long necks when they crow. And you no doubt recall that the hens in *Who Killed Cock Robin?* were unusually well developed and looked more like dowagers than chickens. When a Disney pullet becomes angry, its feathers fly up and you see the tiny pin feathers on its neck. All of these things are exaggerations, of course, but they are the result of patient drawing and study of the birds in real life.

I had seen most of Disney's cartoons, some of them as many as six times, yet it had never occurred to me that behind these caricatures, which bring delight to young and old, lay such hard, serious labor. The only case on record of anyone's gazing with too solemn eyes at the Disney beasts is that of a Midwestern women's organization which objected to Clarabelle Cow's nudity. So Walt obligingly put a skirt on the bovine lady, and she has worn it ever since.

Ducky took me in to see sketches being photographed in the camera room, and then we went on through a room where a hundred girls were coloring the films. I also peeped into the record room, where sometimes Walt himself appears in the role of a recording artist, for he still does the voice for Mickey Mouse.

Actually, Ducky told me, you are likely to find Disney almost anywhere—in an artist's room, snatching a piece of paper and pencil to illustrate an idea; in the directors' room, laughing and kidding with his associates as they work out new stunts; or in the writers' department, looking over a man's shoulder to suggest a new twist.

It was almost six o'clock when word came that Disney would see me. Everybody else had gone home. And there he was in a huge office, the walls of which are covered with medals and certificates from a score of foreign governments. Clad in an out-at-the-elbows smoking jacket, Walt was sitting in a swivel chair, feet cocked on the desk. The first thing about him that impressed me was that his eyes are like the eyes of Mickey Mouse—big, warm, and witty.

"Tell me," I began, "—how do you do it?"

"Well, shall I give it to you a little at a time," he asked, "or do you want it all at once? But seriously," he added, without waiting for an answer, "it's just this:

"We're an organization of young men. We have licked every mechanical difficulty which our medium presented. We don't have to answer to anyone. We don't have to make profits for stockholders. New York investors can't tell us what kind of picture they want us to make or hold back. I get the boys together and we decide what we want to do next. Now it's my ambition to set up the organization so that it will belong to the people in it. The revenue from *Snow White* gives us a chance to go ahead.

"Our greatest hope is that *Bambi* and *Pinocchio*, our next feature-length pictures, will be regarded as highly by the public as *Snow White* has been."

Bambi, © Disney Enterprises, Inc.

In response to my questions, Disney told me how he had gone through school, got a job in an advertising agency, and finally settled down to making movie cartoons. Mrs. Disney was also a cartoonist, and the pair of them were practically starving when the break came. One point which I had long wondered about is why Walt, a Chicago-born youngster, should be so hipped on animals. Everything he has produced has had animals and birds and flowers and trees in it. So I asked him about this interest of his in nature.

"I haven't always lived in a city," he explained. "When I was five my family moved out of Chicago and we went to Marceline, Missouri, where my father had bought a farm. We lived there six years, and I guess it must have made a deep impression on me. I can clearly remember every detail—just as if it had been yesterday. I even remember the train ride from Chicago to Marceline, and I remember the new things that I saw as I looked out of the window. You see, I had never been to the country before.

"When we got off the train we crossed the railroad tracks and went over to a grain elevator and waited for the neighbor who was to meet us.

"Finally we got into a wagon and drove out to the farm. It was a pretty farm with a good house and a big yard. Later we had all sorts of animals—pigs and cows and chickens and ducks and a horse named Charlie. All of us kids would climb on old Charlie's back, and he would head straight for the apple orchard and a tree with very low branches. Then we'd all have to scramble off Charlie's back pretty fast. I also used to ride on an old sow's back, but she'd usually make for the pond, and I frequently ended up in the water.

"Those were the happiest days of my life," Walt continued. "And maybe that's why I go in for country cartoons. Gosh, I hated to leave it—but we had to. The place was sold at auction, and I remember how terrible my brother Roy and I felt as we went about the countryside tacking up signs announcing the sale of our furniture and stuff.

"Not long ago I went back to Marceline and walked out to the old farm. There were circus posters on the barn which we had always kept nice and clean. The house was shabby and unpainted—not clean and white as it was when we lived there. I remember that because of the bawling out I got from my mother when I used some lamp soot paint to draw pictures on the siding.

"I also was reminded of my unhappy adventure with an owl. It was sitting on the low branch of a tree as I crept up behind it and made a grab. The bird, half-blinded by the daylight, whirled on me and nearly scared me to death. In my terror I stamped on the owl and killed it. I've never forgotten that poor bird, and maybe that has something to do with my liking for animals.

"I think that everything you do has some effect on you, and that old farm certainly made an impression on me. I don't know a lot about farming, but when I see a drawing of a pig or a duck or a rooster I know immediately if it has the right feeling. And I know it because of what I learned during those days on the farm."

Walt's first years as a commercial artist, he told me, were spent in drawing eggs and chickens and cows for farm paper advertisements. Mickey Mouse, however, was city bred. Mickey lived in a hole in the wall of Disney's office and shared Walt's midnight snacks with him.

Then Disney told me of his four-year-old daughter, whom he described as his severest critic. She sees most of Disney's films before they're released, and if she likes them, Papa knows they're good.

"How does it feel to be a celebrity?" I asked Walt.

"As far as I can see," he replied, grinning, "being a celebrity has never helped me make a better picture or a good shot in a polo game or command the obedience of my daughter or impress my wife. It doesn't even seem to help keep the fleas off our dogs, and if being a celebrity won't even give you an advantage over a couple of fleas, then I guess there can't be much in being a celebrity after all!"

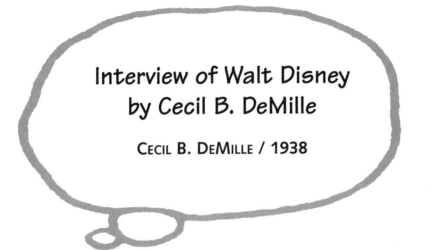

Interview of Walt Disney by Cecil B. DeMille

CECIL B. DEMILLE / 1938

From Lux Radio Theater, CBS,
December 26, 1938. Reprinted courtesy of CBS.

Cecil: In making your pictures do you follow any ironclad rules?
Walt: Just one. Never do anything that someone else can do better. That's why we ordinarily sidestep stories that could be done successfully in live action instead of animated action.

Cecil: What about the future? As the art of animating human figures develops.
Walt: We'll never do *Hamlet*.

Cecil: Wanta bet?
Walt: Well, to be honest, our medium is so young and so unexplored and fascinating that we have to guard against daydreaming. We have too many immediate problems, and I think my most immediate problem is to let you get back to the play.

Cecil: Tell me, just how old a story is "Snow White and the Seven Dwarfs"?

Walt: Well, it's so old that no one knows when or where it was first told.

Cecil: Is it true it wasn't published until the Grimm Brothers came along?

Walt: Yes, just about a hundred years ago. Jacob Grimm was a very learned man, a scientist. You'd hardly think he'd go in for fairy tales. But just as a hobby, he and his brother collected a lot of old folk stories and legends, put them into a book, and called the book, *Grimm's Fairy Tales.*

Cecil: In their written form, Walt, fairy tales are supposedly only for children. But when you bring one to the screen, it captivates everyone. Age, language, race, make no difference. What's the secret?

Walt: Well, here's half an answer. Over at our place, we're sure of just one thing. Everybody in the world was once a child. We grow up. Our personalities change, but in every one of us something remains of our childhood.

Cecil: You mean that's the common denominator?

Walt: That just about sums it up, Mr. DeMille. The same level you speak of knows nothing of sophistication and distinction. It's where all of us are simple and naive without prejudice and bias. We're friendly and trusting and it just seems to me that if your picture hits that spot in one person, it's going to hit the same spot in almost everybody. So, in planning a new picture, we don't think of grown-ups and we don't think of children, but just of that fine, clean, unspoiled spot down deep in every one of us that maybe the world has made us forget and that maybe our pictures can help recall. But when a picture maker turns philosopher, Mr. DeMille, it's time for him to quit. So thanks for your swell treatment of *Snow White and the Seven Dwarfs*. Goodnight.

Talk Given by Walt to All Disney Employees

WALT DISNEY / 1941

From the Walt Disney Archives.

A lot of fellows wonder why we have to have the new Studio. I feel that we are fortunate that we have this new Studio, and *believe me* when I say that it is actually *cheaper* to operate our present organization in the new Studio than it was in the old ones.

Regarding the moving of the buildings from Hyperion, let me say that the quicker we move all usable buildings off the Hyperion lot and completely dismantle it, the quicker we will save money, because taxes and the necessity of watchmen over there are costing the Studio dough.

Some people think that we have class distinction in this place. They wonder why some get better seats in the theater than others. They wonder why some men get spaces in the parking lot and others can't. I have always felt, and always will feel, that the men who are contributing the most to the organization should, out of respect alone, enjoy some privileges. I have tried to be democratic about everything that I have done. If I had the money, I would gladly enlarge the parking space. That is the reason we have instituted a charge of 20¢ a week for parking, and those who are not willing to spend 20¢ a week for a parking space can then park wherever they can find a place.

The preferential seats in the theater usually go to the men who have the most to do with the creative end of the business—the men who make it possible for the others to have jobs.

The Penthouse Club is not a closed thing. We would be glad to allow any fellow who is decent and respectable to belong to it. However, at the start we had to allow those men who carry the main responsibilities of the Studio the first chance to join. After giving those men their chance, we then threw it open to the whole group.

Seniority rights seems to be a great topic of discussion. I hold that seniority does not necessarily mean the length of time a man has been employed, but his ability to contribute as well. All things being equal, a man who had been here longer would have a right to first choice.

Definitely there is no "closed circle." Those men who have worked closely with me in trying to organize and keep this studio rolling, and keep its chin above water, should not be envied. Frankly, those fellows catch plenty of hell, and a lot of you can feel lucky that you don't have too much contact with me.

Another thing that is bothering many people is, "Why so many policemen?" The wage and hour law says that they can't work over forty hours. Nobody in this place ever worked over forty-five hours in the past twelve years, except in emergencies. However, you can rest assured that we don't have too many policemen. They are vitally necessary, and I can assure you that the lowered insurance costs made possible by this adequate protection more than balance the expense. You might also be interested to know that the fireman is required by the insurance.

Another thing, the New York office that we maintain is very vital to our existence. Its entire cost is charged to distribution, and our deal with RKO for distribution is so good that the combined cost of distribution is far less than any other producer in the business can secure.

Regarding certain executives connected with the Studio, the same three men who handled the business affairs of this Studio six years ago are still handling it, and they are Roy Disney, George Morris, and Gunther Lessing. Regarding certain executives' salaries, the highest salaried man in this Studio today is myself. My salary is $500.00 per week.

If I had chosen to take another course, I could easily be making five times that amount. As long as we have been in business, I have never received the salary that was credited to me. When the reorganization and the issue of preferred stock came out, all the back salary credited to my account was wiped out and turned into common stock.

I have never been interested in personal gain or profit. This business and this studio have been my entire life.

The second highest salary in this studio is $350.00 per week, and there is one man who receives that. Roy's salary is $350.00 a week, and nobody can deny him that, because he has been working and slaving and ruining his health for every one of you. Roy knows his business; Roy is doing a marvelous job; and I take my hat off to him.

Another ugly rumor is that we are trying to develop girls for animation to replace higher-priced men. This is the silliest thing I have ever heard of. We are not interested in low-priced help. We are interested in efficient help. Maybe an explanation of why we are training the girls is in order. First, I would like to qualify it with this—that if a woman can do the work as well, she is worth as much as a man.

The girls are being trained for inbetweens for very good reasons. The first is, to make them more versatile, so that the peak loads of inbetweening and inking can be handled. Believe me when I say that the more versatile our organization is, the more beneficial it is to the employees, for it assures steady employment for the employee, as well as steady production turnover for the Studio.

The second reason is that the possibility of a war, let alone the peacetime conscription, may take many of our young men now employed, and especially many of the young applicants. I believe that if there is to be a business for these young men to come back to after the war, it must be maintained during the war. The girls can help here.

Third, the girl artists have the right to expect the same chances for advancement as men, and I honestly believe that they may eventually contribute something to this business that men never would or could. In the present group that are training for inbetweens there are definite prospects, and a good example is to mention the work of Ethel Kulsar and Sylvia Holland on *The Nutcracker Suite*, and little Rhetta Scott, of whom you will hear more when you see *Bambi*.

There is another rumor to the effect that we are trying to develop a lot of low-priced animators to hold down wages. This is not only ridiculous but, I believe, vicious. A man learning a business, trying to progress, can't get anywhere unless he is given an opportunity. You can't pay a man a salary until he proves that he can earn it. If an assistant getting $50.00 a week gets a chance to animate, to prove himself an animator, the plan in operation in this Studio is that that man, at $50.00 a week, gets a chance to prove himself on the same footage cost scale as a man earning $300.00 a week. Facts prove that it usually turns out that the man getting $50.00 a week costs the studio more per foot than the man getting $300.00. If he doesn't cost them more, then he gets the difference. What could be fairer?

Here is a question that is asked many times, and about which I think a complete misunderstanding exists. I will try my best to set it straight. The question it: "Why can't Walt see more of the fellows? Why can't there be less supervisors and more Walt?"

The first very good reason is that the day is too short. Have you ever thought of it in this way—if the organization was small enough for me to work with and have contact with all the men, it would have to be a rather small organization; because after all, I'm only one guy, and I'm only human. Such an organization would probably be capable of producing twelve shorts a year. That means that only a handful of one hundred people or so would be necessary. Now simple mathematics leaves eleven hundred people who are here at the present time, who would not be here under such a setup.

Another reason is this—in the early days I tried to be very democratic. It's my nature to be democratic. I want to be just a guy working in this plant—which I am. When I meet people in the hall I want to be able to speak to them, and have them speak back to me, and say "hello" with a smile. I can't work under any other conditions. However, I realized at that time that it was very dangerous and unfair to the organization as a whole for me to get too close to everybody. This was especially true of new men. You all know that there are always those who try to polish the apple, or to get their advancement by playing on sympathy. It is obvious that this is definitely unfair to the conscientious, hard-working individual who is not good at apple-polishing. I know, and am well aware of the progress of all the men after they reach a certain spot in this organization. Some of them I might not recognize when I meet them, but I know them by name and reputation. Believe me, when a fellow shows something, I hear about it; and not through any central source but by a general contact with all the key men in the organization. And fellows, I take my hat off to results only.

Another very important point regarding this same matter is this: It is my belief that if this is to be a strong, self-sufficient organization, it cannot be run by one man. I do not want this organization set up so that it would not function without me, merely to please my ego. This organization must perpetuate itself; it must be able to carry on if anything should ever happen to me. The future of all the men who have given their time and effort to this business cannot be jeopardized by any selfish attitude on my part, or any desire to be the big shot. We have constantly been searching for leaders; we have made many mistakes, and have tried to rectify those mistakes. While training artists and technicians, we have at the same time been trying to train executives. We have been trying to find men who could be recognized as leaders not by the wearing of a badge, but by the respect of their fellow-workers. We need those men to carry this business on. A policy and a plan like this assures a strong solid organization that can rise to any emergency; and above all, and perhaps the most important thing, is that it means security to every man here.

Mr. and Mrs. Disney

LADIES' HOME JOURNAL / 1941

From *Ladies' Home Journal*, LVIII,
March 1941, pp. 20, 146. Compilation
© 1941 in *Ladies' Home Journal*,
Meredith Corporation.

"Look," the fellow in the wine-colored trousers, collarless shirt and
scuffed moccasins was saying to Leopold Stokowski and Deems Taylor
in one of the cork-lined conference rooms of Walt Disney Productions'
fabulous new studio, "I really don't know beans about music."

The $2,000,000 production *Fantasia*, designed to visualize, animate
and interpret a two-and-a-half-hour concert by Stokowski and the
Philadelphia Orchestra, was just getting under way. The conductor
looked at Deems Taylor, who looked the other way.

"That's all right, Walt," genial-voiced Taylor said soothingly. "When
I first started, I thought Bach wrote love stuff—like Romeo and Juliet.
You know, I thought maybe Toccata was in love with Fugue."

Walt roared. He knew all about Bach's Toccata and Fugue in D Minor. It was going to be in the picture. "Say, let's hear Beethoven's Sixth Symphony again," he said to the man standing by a phonograph. And then, a few minutes later, "You know, I think this picture will make Beethoven."

Stokowski hesitated a moment. Then, "That's right, Walt," he agreed. "In a certain sense, it will. Some who have never heard his name will see this."

And they have. Millions right now are flocking to *Fantasia*, to be shaken to their shoes and thrilled to the core by the teeth-gnashing, soul-storming cyclonic interpretations of Disney, who, although no musicologist, is one of the most musically sensitive people Stokowski says he's ever known. And Deems Taylor, vitriolic in his condemnation of the so-called "dowager" program notes for concerts, long-winded affairs explaining the music measure by measure, couldn't be more elated over Disney's dynamically fresh interpretations. All except for one little thing.

"I Like everything except the centaurs in Beethoven's Pastoral Symphony," he says, and adds, a bit wistfully, "They should look more like lifeguards."

Fantasia, © Disney Enterprises, Inc.

This musical master, genius of the animated cartoon, Walt Disney, is a living testimonial to the importance of moderation in education, including music-appreciation courses. Disney attended school in both Kansas City and Chicago, but at the end of his first year in high school, suspecting that things had gone far enough, he quit, and it is doubtful whether he has cracked a book since. This left him with an unsophisticated viewpoint highly sympathetic to that of his future audiences, and made it possible for him to be active in his lifework at an age when his less thoughtful contemporaries were, if they were lucky, still being voted the second wittiest men in their classes.

Disney's intransigent attitude toward the intermediate and higher learning has softened somewhat since June, 1938, when he consented, on successive days, to accept honorary degrees from Harvard and Yale, but he is no campus fool. He is convinced that the New Haven award was largely an occasion trumped up to enable Billy Phelps, who made the presentation citation, to get off a gag about Disney laboring like a mountain and bringing forth a mouse, but as a gag man himself this has only increased his appreciation of the event. Recipient, in the past six or seven years, of enough certificates to turn the head of a dentist, he meets college graduates without any hint of condescension, and frequently hires them without the slightest suggestion of prejudice because their degrees have been won in a routine, unimaginative way.

Animated cartoons had for so many years been regarded as a stepchild of the motion-picture industry that Disney's Eastern degrees, bestowed in recognition of the merits of *Snow White and the Seven Dwarfs*, the world's first feature-length cartoon in color, came as something of a surprise to the Hollywood community. The live-action people were further jogged when New York's Metropolitan Museum of Art secured a painted still of the vultures in *Snow White*. The thing that is really making Hollywood sit up and take notice, however, is the flood of unimpeachable million-dollar statistics that are beginning to come out of the Disney office. *Snow White*, for example, cost $2,400,000 to make and market, and has grossed over $8,000,000—$4,000,000 in the United States, the rest in forty-five other countries. *Pinocchio* earned some $2,000,000 and *Fantasia* may even surpass *Snow White's* receipts.

Disney still affects a mild surprise at large figures, however. A friend who dropped in at his office last August found him studying a report from his brother, Roy, who is actively in charge of the financial side of the business. "Gee!" he said. "Since October we've spent $3,277,000."

The Disneys live comparatively modestly in a twelve-room house in the Silver Lake district, a section inhabited by Los Angeles businessmen rather than motion-picture people. Walt likes to roughhouse with his daughters, Diane Marie, eight, and four-year-old Sharon Mae, who is adopted; to act out scenes from such future projects as *Bambi, Alice in Wonderland* and the birth of Jesus Christ to get the reactions of his wife, an Idaho girl named Lillian Bounds, who worked in his studio before their marriage. The studio at that time was a garage, and Disney was in need of an assistant. When this dark-haired, vivacious girl appeared in answer to his ad, Disney hired her on the spot, and married her soon afterward. They've been married sixteen years now, and friends are likely to point out it's one of the happiest—if least publicized—marriages in Hollywood.

She and Walt both like family get-togethers, and a Sunday group at their home is likely to include such assorted Disneys as Walt's father, his Uncle Robert, Roy and two other brothers, Raymond and Herbert, who are an insurance broker and a mailman, respectively. Ray Disney handles Walt's $750,000 policy and all the insurance for Disney employees, but Herbert, the eldest of the four brothers—Walt is the youngest—has no connection with the business. Roy and Walt have offered to take him in, but Herbert feels that the fresh air which his calling enables him to breathe is healthier for him; and moreover, he is in line for a pension in a few years. The Disneys are all homespun, unpretentious people and they consider Herbert's stand perfectly sensible.

Although, at the studio, Walt Disney is the ultimate authority on all the steps of making a cartoon, he does no drawing or painting himself. He is admittedly a wretched draftsman, and it is not at all likely that he could get a job in his own animation department, even with all his pull. This is a source of occasional discomfiture to him, as when autograph hunters and dinner partners ask him for a sketch of Mickey Mouse as a souvenir. On a trip to Europe a few years ago he considerately took along a sheaf of Mickey Mouse sketches by one of his animators, and palmed them off as original Disneys to insistent acquaintances. The fact that his employees rarely get public credit for their work is the result of a policy calculated to prevent interoffice jealousy rather than a desire on Disney's part to hog the show. It was at his suggestion that the credit for the picture bought by the Metropolitan Museum was amplified from "Walt Disney" to "Walt Disney and Staff."

Despite an inability to draw as well as most of his staff, Walt Elias Disney early fooled his family into thinking he was going to become an artist in the usual sense of the word. On one occasion he covered their farmhouse with figures painted with tar he had dug out of a barrel. Convinced of the prophetic nature of these daubs, an aunt plied him with art books. He responded by producing more drawings, many of which were snapped up by a neighboring horse doctor.

When Disney was eight his parents moved to Kansas City. Around this time he developed another talent, the ability to act, which has turned out much better than his drawing. In 1913 Kansas City was a hive of Chaplin-impersonation contests.

"I'd get in line with half a dozen guys," he says. "I'd ad lib and play with my cane and gloves. Sometimes I'd win $5, sometimes $2.50, sometimes just get carfare. I made the wig out of old hemp used to stuff pipes; it stunk of creosote. Later I got wise to crepe hair."

According to Alva Johnston, a student of the period, Disney was the second-best Chaplin in Kansas City. His theatrical career never got much farther than this, but he still likes to act things out, and his conversation is punctuated with expressive gestures and facial contortions. He likes other people to talk this way also, and is distressed because his brother Roy, a tireless listener, is a nonhistrionic conversationalist.

"Roy's patience sometimes gets on my nerves," he says. "I like people to jump and shout with enthusiasm."

Disney's powers of impersonation came in handy during the war. Rejected by the Red Cross because he was only sixteen, he went home, assumed a more mature expression, came back and impersonated a man of eighteen and was accepted. When his father asked him why he wanted to go to war, he said, "When my children ask me what I did in the war, I want to be able to say I was in it." Disney's elder daughter, Diane, is only eight, and hasn't asked him yet, but he keeps bringing the war up in conversation in a hopeful sort of way.

He helped evacuate hospitals abroad, and continued his career of artistic deception by pretending to the other Red Cross men that he knew how to draw. The Snow White spirit was already strong in him, and he declined flattering offers to portray off-color subjects. He was not above shooting craps, however, and by the time he returned in the fall of 1919 he had so augmented his capital by this means that he was worth $500.

His family wanted him to go back to school, but Disney felt it was preposterous for a man with $500 to be at school, and got a job driving a truck instead. This was soon followed by a ten-dollar-a-week position drawing advertisements for farm journals. Laid off after Christmas, he worked briefly as a postman, and then went into the commercial-art business with a friend.

A couple of months later, by answering a want ad, Disney got a job making animated cartoons for the Kansas City Slide Company. He got several friends who knew how to draw to work with him evenings, and they produced a short on the subject of Little Red Ridinghood. Disney resigned from the slide company when he was twenty-one and formed a corporation which produced several modernized children's stories. A year later his distributing agency went into bankruptcy. It failed to pay Disney for his films and left him $15,000 in debt.

Disney decided to start life afresh in Hollywood, where his brother Roy and an uncle, Robert Disney, were living. Backed by their uncle, a real-estate operator, he and Roy opened a studio and made a series of pictures called *Alice in Cartoonland*, in which a real girl moved against a background of cartoon figures. They got an Eastern distributor and imported a staff of several Kansas City cartoonists. Alice was followed by Oswald, the Rabbit, and this was so successful that when Disney asked his distributor for more money the latter raided Disney's staff and proceeded to make Oswald himself, without benefit of Disney.

Bereft of his rabbit, his staff, but not his senses, Disney decided to make a mouse his hero. He had long had a high regard for mice, and in Kansas City kept several of the little creatures in a large box.

About this time he and the very pretty Miss Bounds met, fell in love and presently—in July 1925—were married. With Mrs. Disney's help, Walt made two silent Mickey Mouse shorts, neither of which sold. The third Mickey Mouse, a sound affair called *Steamboat Willie*, opened in New York in the fall of 1928 and was wildly successful. Next came the first Silly Symphony, *The Skeleton Dance*, which was also a popular success, although many theaters rejected it as too gruesome.

Disney takes an innocent pleasure in the grisly, and his colleagues are sometimes at pains to make him tone down macabre pieces of business. Nevertheless, a certain code of conduct has evolved for Disney characters. If they indulge in gunfire, bullets must glance off, not penetrate. As a general thing no animal may be killed. "A chicken can eat a worm if we haven't had a close-up of the worm to show he has character," a member of Disney's staff explained recently.

Although Disney is naturally a modest fellow, he has made something of a cult of his simplicity. He drives to work in a blue coupé and was full of apologies when it leaked out that he also has a bigger car in which a chauffeur sometimes drives him around. He once cut off his mustache after reading in a magazine that a mustache is a sign of conceit, and although he grew it again it is this point of view that prompted his Uncle Robert to say, "I give Walt credit for holding himself just like a real sensible fellow would. He hasn't swelled up a bit."

He took up polo a few years ago, and used to play a good deal at the Riviera Country Club with Will Rogers, Spencer Tracy and others, but soon gave it up, partly because he felt it was too expensive and partly because he fell so often that his staff persuaded him his life—and their livelihood— was in danger. He gets most of his exercise from badminton, taking rumba lessons, doing gym work, and jumping around while conversing.

He is called "Walt" by all his employees except Mr. Rogers, the studio carpenter, who calls him "Mr. Disney." Mr. Rogers, an elderly man, is one of the few people over forty in the studio, and Disney reciprocates by calling him "Mr. Rogers."

This easy camaraderie—this complete lack of red tape, titles, dignity—goes a long way to explain the success of Walt Disney Productions, Inc. This, plus the prodigious imagination of its originator, his equally prodigious mania for detail.

One day, when *Fantasia* was almost completed, Disney was discussing with Deems Taylor a cover drawing for the music critic's new book on *Fantasia*.

"Look, Deems," Walt pointed out. "How are you going to put the title on the back binding?"

"Well"—Taylor hesitated—"I really hadn't thought—"

"The point is," Walt went on, "how are people going to put this in their bookcases? Now, it's a big book, over twelve inches high, too big for most bookshelves. That means people are going to lay it on its side. I think you'd better put the name at right angles to the title on the front, so they'll be able to read it. . . . And now, Stoki," he said, turning to the conductor, "about that fifth dewdrop fairy in the Tchaikovsky number. . . ."

That Million-Dollar Mouse

FRANK NUGENT / 1947

From the *New York Times Magazine,*
September 21, 1947, pp. 22, 60.

Twenty years ago a man labored and brought forth a mouse and the civilized world still hasn't stopped applauding the miracle. Mickey Mouse is the goshdarndest single act of creation in the history of our civilization. He probably is more widely known than any President, King, artist, actor, poet, composer or tycoon who ever lived. The worlds that Alexander the Great conquered and Julius Caesar ruled were nutshell microcosms compared with that over which Mickey holds sway. His sovereignty is all but universal, yet he is as American as Kansas City; he was born on a westbound Pullman and his harried parent, Walt Disney, can't for the life of him remember exactly when or where. It was "somewhere out of Chicago," and there wasn't a midwife on the train.

It was to the Disney studio in Burbank—the $2,000,000 plant which Mickey built—that I went last week for a first-hand account of the creation and development of Walt's colossal mouse.

Most Hollywood studios look like storage warehouses: Disney's mulberry-and-green layout is more of a cross between a country club and a sanitarium. It has a baseball diamond, a battery of pingpong tables, a couple of horseshoe-pitching lanes and a penthouse sun-deck where the male employees acquire an all-over tan. The workaday buildings are air-conditioned and reasonably dustproof. Walt's office suite has a stainless steel kitchen, a dressing room and shower, a piano, radio-phonograph, couches, coffee tables and a desk which has acquired an inferiority complex through his consistent disuse of it.

"I want to interview Mickey," I said, taking the mouse by the horns.

Walt looked down his nose at me.

"I dunno," he said. "It's a little irregular. We've kinda frowned on direct interviews. The Mouse's private life isn't especially colorful. He's never been the type that would go in for swimming pools and night clubs; more the simple country boy at heart. Lives on a quiet residential street, has occasional dates with his girl friend, Minnie, doesn't drink or smoke, likes the movies and band concerts, things like that."

"I'd still like to ask him some questions," I said firmly.

Walt's fingers drubbed the desk. His employees recognize it as a danger signal, once removed from his rubbing the side of his nose with a straight index finger. But I wasn't on the payroll so I just waited.

"I've always done The Mouse's talking," Walt said. [He never calls Mickey by his first name; he's always The Mouse just as Donald is always The Duck]. "He's a shy little feller, so I've provided the voice. I use a falsetto, like this. [And he demonstrated.] His voice changed after I had my tonsils out. It became a little deeper. But no one noticed it. I kind of like it better. Sometimes I'm sorry I started the voice. It takes a lot of time and I feel silly doing The Mouse in front of the sound crew.

"But I'm sentimental about him, I guess, and it wouldn't be the same if anyone else did the speaking. We've had several girls for Minnie. The original got married and had a couple of kids and that was that. What sort of questions?"

Was Mickey born in an upper berth or a lower? Did he spring full-grown onto a drawing pad, and how about his family background? How tall is he, what's his attitude toward Donald Duck, how much does he make a year, any chance of his retirement, how does he stand politically?

"One at a time," said Walt. "He was born in a section. Things weren't *that* tough. But it wasn't a good train. I remember there was no diner and we stopped for meals, I was going to call him Mortimer Mouse, but my wife suggested 'Mickey' and that sounded better.

"Now he's Mikki Maus in Russia, Miki Kuchi in Japan, Miguel Ratoncito in Spanish-speaking countries, Michel Souris in France and Topolino in Italy.

"Sure he was born full-grown, but he wasn't fully developed. That took a lot of time—twenty years so far. He'll probably keep on developing. Why don't you look at some of his early pictures and talk to the boys? Then you'll see how he's changed through the years."

The Disney family album is a film storage vault. In it are the 118 shorts Mickey has appeared in since *Steamboat Willie* opened at the Colony Theatre exactly nineteen years ago today. In it, also, are Mickey's two features, *Fantasia* and the current *Fun and Fancy Free*. Technically, *Steamboat Willie* was the first Mickey Mouse cartoon; actually two others, *Plane Crazy* and *Galloping Gaucho*, had been made before it, but sound had come in meanwhile and the two silent shorts were held back

Steamboat Willie, © Disney Enterprises, Inc.

while *Willie* got the benefit of synchronization—though by today's perfectionist standards, it wasn't much of a benefit. The sound seems to come from some place ten years behind the screen. Still Mickey makes you forget that. Even then he had personality.

But he wasn't the Mickey we know now. His legs were pipestems and he had only black dots for eyes. His muzzle and nose were longer and so was his tail. He was thinner and more angular then and his movements were on the jerky side. His acting was influenced by the Keystone Comedy school; he would jump in the air before starting to run and when an idea dawned you could see it climbing the horizon. He indulged in some cruelties and crudities that would shock his fans today—like pulling a cat's tail and using a goose as a bagpipe while playing a one-man band.

The projectionist turned the pages of the family album rapidly. There was Mickey as a convict in *Chain Gang* in 1930; among the prisoners were two hounds—one of them later became Pluto. Mickey shared the stage and spotlight with an irascible duck in *The Orphan's Benefit* in 1934; Donald had made his bow as a heavy in a Silly Symphony called *The Wise Little Hen* a few months before, but it was as the frustrated reciter of "Little Boy Blue" that he really wowed 'em.

Somewhere in the late thirties Mickey lost his tail; a canny production man had figured that thousands of dollars would be saved by not having to animate that eloquent little appendage. But Mickey didn't seem the same without it and the tail was restored.

Mickey acquired color in *The Band Concert* in 1935 and never has reverted to black and white. As the mouse grew older his black-dot eyes were replaced with expressive, rollable eyeballs. He began wearing "longies" to hide the pipestem legs and the stems themselves thickened. He gained a little weight and acquired a flexible body. His knees and elbows lost their angularity.

But the most important development was in his acting ability. He learned to emote without calisthenics and, with that advance, the basic character of the Mickey Mouse comedies underwent a radical change. Instead of the slapdash chases and slapstick climaxes of *The Fire Chief* and *Building a Building*, Mickey began giving us the gentler comedy, tinged with pathos, of *Brave Little Tailor*. He became a situation comedian, not just a funny man—or mouse; a Harold Lloyd, say, rather than a Chaplin—or a Donald Duck.

No one can tell at Disney's—Walt least of all—just to what extent Mickey is a self-made mouse. Artists like Fred Moore, Marvin Woodward,

Les Clark and Kenny Muse have helped him to express himself. They taught him a lot of tricks—how to let his shoulders droop and his feet drag when he is despondent, how to strut on his way to a date with Minnie, how to convey by an eye-brow's lift an emotion that he used to project by leaping a yard in the air. But not even Disney can explain why he sometimes sits with his story men and solemnly asks: "But would The Mouse do a thing like that?" And if the conclave decides that he wouldn't, then out it goes—no matter how funny the gag.

The modern Mickey—they now know—wouldn't pull a cat's tail to make music and couldn't be found on a chain gang without there being some innocent explanation of it. Mickey is ringed about with musts and must-nots. In addition to not smoking and not drinking, he doesn't use any language stronger than a "shucks."

Donald has no such limitations; he can be diabolic even to the point of looting his nephews' piggy bank. Some of the heretics at Disney's will confide that they have more fun working with the duck than with the mouse for just this reason and hint that the public's current preference for Donald over Mickey (the Gallup Audience Research Institute puts Donald first, Bugs Bunny second and Mickey third) is a vote for human fallibility.

Walt only smiled wisely when I brought this treasonable report to his office. "Sure," he admitted. "After 120 pictures, it's only natural for them to get a little tired of The Mouse. It's tough to come up with new ideas, to keep him fresh and at the same time in character. The Duck's a lot easier. You can do anything with him. But what they forget is that The Mouse hasn't made a picture since the war. He was in one short released in '42. Five years off the screen and he still rates third! Is there any star in Hollywood with a public that loyal?"

Then it was safe to state—I ventured—that Mickey is not jealous of the upstart duck?

"His attitude," replied Walt pontifically, "is that of the older master who's glad to give the youngsters a hand. After all, this is a big place and there's room for everybody. The Mouse knows we have to keep bringing new people along, new faces. It makes his job that much easier. It was pretty tough when he was carrying the whole studio. But now he's got The Duck and Pluto and The Goof and our feature program. Quite an accomplishment for a mouse."

Walt wouldn't tell me about Mickey's politics, except to say that they do not resemble Chaplin's, and he was a bit vague when I tried to find out exactly how tall the mouse was. The best I could get was that he's three quarters the size of the goof, about a head taller than the duck, and a third bigger than Pluto. He stands about even with the coloratura, Clara Cluck, and is exactly level with Minnie—which may be due to the fact that Minnie originally was Mickey with eyelashes, a skirt and feminine footgear; otherwise the drawing was identical.

"What's he make a year?" I asked.

"What year?" countered Walt, and stopped me cold.

"Well, what's he made in all, over the twenty years?" I asked finally.

"Me," Walt said and I had to let it go at that.

Kay Kamen was more specific. Mr. Kamen is the Kansas City advertising man who has been Disney's licensing agent since 1932. He is the middleman between Walt and the thousand-and-one manufacturers and advertisers who use the Disney characters on their products.

The Disney label, says Mr. Kamen, helps to sell about $100,000,000 worth of goods each year and Mickey is the best salesman of the lot. Books are the chief item, going at the rate of 10,000,000 a year and ranging in price from kindergarten primers at $1 a copy to a deluxe Deems Taylor edition of *Fantasia* at $3.75. A Walt Disney Illustrated *Uncle Remus* ran through a first printing of 150,000 in practically no time and another is on the presses. The Walt Disney Comics, a monthly comic-strip magazine, sells to the merry tune of 30,000,000 a year and rates fourth on newsstand sales of all national magazines.

Mickey is a consistent salesman of cereals, soaps, dolls, toys, sweaters, sweatshirts, phonographs and records, radios, hot-water bottles, hairbrushes, caps, robes, slippers, footballs, baseballs, paint sets, porringers and, most notably, the Mickey Mouse watches—600,000 of them sold so far this year.

A Los Angeles ceramics plant stacks its kilns exclusively with Disney figurines; one of the nation's largest doll manufacturers gives Mickey top priority. A New York department store sold $10,000 worth of Disney-decorated sweaters in a day.

No small-time operator, Mickey has made tie-ups with Standard Oil, General Foods, Standard Brands, National Biscuit Company, DuPont and National Dairy Products. He has declined bids from liquor companies, cigarette manufacturers, makers of patent medicines.

The net income to Disney from all these sidelines has been, Mr. Kamen estimates, from $500,000 to $800,000 a year. "No doubt of it," says Mr. Kamen, "Mickey Mouse is the greatest thing in the history of merchandising."

What this means to the mouse himself, how it affects his standard of living, whether he is any closer now to being able to support a wife called Minnie than he was twenty years ago, what kind of a car he drives, what he thinks of screen vs. stage and his opinion of the English tax on Hollywood films are, unfortunately, questions I have been unable to clear up satisfactorily.

I can only add that as I left Walt's office, I heard behind me the sounds of a drawer rattling in that unused desk and then a voice in a familiar falsetto. "It's the next birthday that worries me," it said. "Tell me, boss: When I'm 21 will I be a man, or a mouse?" I dashed back into the room. Walt looked up in surprise.

"I thought I heard something," I explained.

"Probably a mouse," he said, and went on working.

The Testimony of Walter E. Disney Before the House Committee on Un-American Activities

ROBERT E. STRIPLING AND H. A. SMITH / 1947

From the House Committee on Un-American Activities, October 24, 1947. Reprinted in *The American Animated Cartoon* by Danny Peary and Gerald Peary (New York: Dutton, 1980, pp. 92–98).

[ROBERT E.] STRIPLING [CHIEF INVESTIGATOR]: Mr. Disney, will you state your full name and present address, please?

WALTER DISNEY: Walter E. Disney, Los Angeles, California.

RES: When and where were you born, Mr. Disney?

WD: Chicago, Illinois, December 5, 1901.

RES: December 5, 1901?

WD: Yes, sir.

RES: What is your occupation?

WD: Well, I am a producer of motion-picture cartoons.

RES: Mr. Chairman, the interrogation of Mr. Disney will be done by
Mr. Smith.

THE CHAIRMAN [J. PARNELL THOMAS]: Mr. Smith.

[H. A.] Smith: Mr. Disney, how long have you been in that business?

WD: Since 1920.

HAS: You have been in Hollywood during this time?

WD: I have been in Hollywood since 1923.

HAS: At the present time you own and operate the Walt Disney Studio
at Burbank, California?

WD: Well, I am one of the owners. Part owner.

HAS: How many people are employed there, approximately?

WD: At the present time about 600.

HAS: And what is the approximate largest number of employees you
have had in the studio?

WD: Well, close to 1,400 at times.

HAS: Will you tell us a little about the nature of this particular studio, the
type of pictures you make, and approximately how many per year?

WD: Well, mainly cartoon films. We make about twenty short subjects,
and about two features a year.

HAS: Will you talk just a little louder, Mr. Disney?

WD: Yes, sir.

HAS: How many, did you say?

WD: About twenty short subject cartoons and about two features
per year.

HAS: And some of the characters in the films consist of—

WD: You mean such as Mickey Mouse and Donald Duck and *Snow
White and the Seven Dwarfs* [1938], and things of that sort.

HAS: Where are these films distributed?

WD: All over the world.

HAS: In all countries of the world?

WD: Well, except the Russian countries.

HAS: Why aren't they distributed in Russia, Mr. Disney?

WD: Well, we can't do business with them.

HAS: What do you mean by that?

WD: Oh, well, we have sold them some films a good many years ago.
They bought the *Three Little Pigs* [1933] and used it through Russia.
And they looked at a lot of our pictures, and I think they ran a lot of
them in Russia, but then turned them back to us and said they didn't
want them, they didn't suit their purposes.

HAS: Is the dialogue in these films translated into the various foreign languages?

WD: Yes. On one film we did ten foreign versions. That was *Snow White and the Seven Dwarfs.*

HAS: Have you ever made any pictures in your studio that contained propaganda and that were propaganda films?

WD: Well, during the war we did. We made quite a few—working with different government agencies. We did one for the Treasury on taxes and I did four anti-Hitler films. And I did one on my own for air power.

HAS: From those pictures that you made, have you any opinion as to whether or not the films can be used effectively to disseminate propaganda?

WD: Yes, I think they proved that.

HAS: How do you arrive at that conclusion?

WD: Well, on the one for the Treasury on taxes, it was to let the people know that taxes were important in the war effort. As they explained to me, they had 13,000,000 new taxpayers, people who had never paid taxes, and they explained that it would be impossible to prosecute all those that were delinquent and they wanted to put this story before those people so they would get their taxes in early. I made the film, and after the film had its run the Gallup poll organization polled the public and the findings were that twenty-nine percent of the people admitted that had influenced them in getting their taxes in early and giving them a picture of what taxes will do.

HAS: Aside from those pictures you made during the war, have you made any other pictures, or do you permit pictures to be made at your studio containing propaganda?

WD: No; we never have. During the war we thought it was a different thing. It was the first time we ever allowed anything like that to go in the films. We watch so that nothing gets into the films that would be harmful in any way to any group or any country. We have large audiences of children and different groups, and we try to keep them as free from anything that would offend anybody as possible. We work hard to see that nothing of that sort creeps in.

HAS: Do you have any people in your studio at the present time that you believe are Communist or Fascist, employed there?

WD: No; at the present time I feel that everybody in my studio is one-hundred-percent American.

HAS: Have you had at any time, in your opinion, in the past, have you at any time in the past had any Communists employed at your studio?

WD: Yes; in the past I had some people that I definitely feel were Communists.

HAS: As a matter of fact, Mr. Disney, you experienced a strike at your studio, did you not?

WD: Yes.

HAS: And is it your opinion that that strike was instituted by members of the Communist Party to serve their purposes?

WD: Well, it proved itself so with time, and I definitely feel it was a Communist group trying to take over my artists and they did take them over.

CHAIRMAN: Do you say they did take them over?

WD: They did take them over.

HAS: Will you explain that to the committee, please?

WD: It came to my attention when a delegation of my boys, my artists, came to me and told me that Mr. Herbert Sorrell—

HAS: Is that Herbert K. Sorrell?

WD: Herbert K. Sorrell, was trying to take them over. I explained to them that it was none of my concern, that I had been cautioned to not even talk with any of my boys on labor. They said it was not a matter of labor, it was just a matter of them not wanting to go with Sorrell, and they had heard that I was going to sign with Sorrell, and they said that they wanted an election to prove that Sorrell didn't have the majority, and I said that I had a right to demand an election. So when Sorrell came, I demanded an election.

Sorrell wanted me to sign on a bunch of cards that he had there that he claimed were the majority, but the other side had claimed the same thing. I told Mr. Sorrell that there is only one way for me to go and that was an election and that is what the law had set up, the National Labor Relations Board was for that purpose. He laughed at me and he said that he would use the Labor Board as it suited his purposes and that he had been sucker enough to go for that Labor Board ballot and he had lost some election—I can't remember the name of the place—by one vote. He said it took him two years to get it back. He said he would strike, that that was his weapon. He said, "I have all of the tools of the trade sharpened," that I couldn't stand the ridicule or the smear of a strike. I told him that it was a matter of principle with me, that I couldn't go on working with my boys feeling that I had sold them down the river to him on his say-so, and he laughed at me and told me I was naïve and foolish. He said, you can't stand this strike, I will smear you, and I will make a dust bowl out of your plant.

CHAIRMAN: What was that?

WD: He said he would make a dust bowl out of my plant if he chose to. I told him I would have to go that way, sorry, that he might be able to do all that, but I would have to stand on that. The result was that he struck.

I believed at that time that Mr. Sorrell was a Communist because of all the things that I had heard and having seen his name appearing on a number of Commie front things. When he pulled the strike, the first people to smear me and put me on the unfair list were all of the Commie front organizations. I can't remember them all, they change so often, but one that is clear in my mind is the League of Women Shoppers, *The People's World, The Daily Worker,* and the *PM* magazine in New York. They smeared me. Nobody came near to find out what the true facts of the thing were. And I even went through the same smear in South America, through some Commie periodicals in South America, and generally throughout the world all of the Commie groups began smear campaigns against me and my pictures.

JOHN MCDOWELL: In what fashion was that smear, Mr. Disney, what type of smear?

WD: Well, they distorted everything, they lied; there was no way you could ever counteract anything that they did; they formed picket lines in front of the theaters, and, well, they called my plant a sweatshop, and that is not true, and anybody in Hollywood would prove it otherwise. They claimed things that were not true at all and there was no way you could fight it back. It was not a labor problem at all because—I mean, I have never had labor trouble, and I think that would be backed up by anybody in Hollywood.

HAS: As a matter of fact, you have how many unions operating in your plant?

CHAIRMAN: Excuse me just a minute. I would like to ask a question.

HAS: Pardon me.

CHAIRMAN: In other words, Mr. Disney, Communists out there smeared you because you wouldn't knuckle under?

WD: I wouldn't go along with their way of operating. I insisted on it going through the National Labor Relations Board. And he told me outright that he used them as it suited his purposes.

CHAIRMAN: Supposing you had given in to him, then what would have been the outcome?

WD: Well, I would never have given in to him, because it was a matter of principle with me, and I fight for principles. My boys have been there, have grown up in the business with me, and I didn't feel like I could sign them over to anybody. They were vulnerable at that time. They were not organized. It is a new industry.

CHAIRMAN: Go ahead, Mr. Smith.

HAS: How many labor unions, approximately, do you have operating in your studios at the present time?

WD: Well, we operate with around thirty-five—I think we have contacts with thirty.

HAS: At the time of this strike you didn't have any grievances or labor troubles whatsoever in your plant?

WD: No. The only real grievance was between Sorrell and the boys within my plant, they demanding an election, and they never got it.

HAS: Do you recall having had any conversations with Mr. Sorrell relative to Communism?

WD: Yes, I do.

HAS: Will you relate that conversation?

WD: Well, I didn't pull my punches on how I felt. He evidently heard that I had called them all a bunch of Communists—and I believe they are. At the meeting he leaned over and he said, "You think I am a Communist, don't you," and I told him that all I knew was what I heard and what I had seen, and he laughed and said, "Well, I used their money to finance my strike of 1937," and he said that he had gotten the money through the personal check of some actor, but he didn't name the actor. I didn't go into it any further. I just listened.

HAS: Can you name any other individuals that were active at the time of the strike that you believe in your opinion are Communists?

WD: Well, I feel that there is one artist in my plant, that came in there, he came in about 1938, and he sort of stayed in the background, he wasn't too active, but he was the real brains of this, and I believe he is a Communist. His name is David Hilberman.

HAS: How is it spelled?

WD: H-i-l-b-e-r-m-a-n, I believe. I looked into his record and I found that, number 1, that he had no religion and, number 2, that he had spent considerable time at the Moscow Art Theatre studying art direction, or something.

HAS: Any others, Mr. Disney?

WD: Well, I think Sorrell is sure tied up with them. If he isn't a Communist, he sure should be one.

HAS: Do you remember the name of William Pomerance, did he have anything to do with it?

WD: Yes, sir. He came in later. Sorrell put him in charge as business manager of cartoonists and later he went to the Screen Actors as their business agent, and in turn he put in another man by the name of Maurice Howard, the present business agent. And they are all tied up with the same outfit.

HAS: What is your opinion of Mr. Pomerance and Mr. Howard as to whether or not they are or are not Communists?

WD: In my opinion they are Communists. No one has any way of proving those things.

HAS: Were you able to produce during the strike?

WD: Yes, I did, because there was a very few, very small majority that was on the outside, and all the other unions ignored all the lines because of the setup of the thing.

HAS: What is your personal opinion of the Communist Party, Mr. Disney, as to whether or not it is a political party?

WD: Well, I don't believe it is a political party. I believe it is an un-American thing. The thing that I resent the most is that they are able to get into these unions, take them over, and represent to the world that a group of people that are in my plant, that I know are good, one-hundred-percent Americans, are trapped by this group, and they are represented to the world as supporting all of those ideologies, and it is not so, and I feel that they really ought to be smoked out and shown up for what they are, so that all of the good, free causes in this country, all the liberalisms that really are American, can go out without the taint of communism. That is my sincere feeling on it.

HAS: Do you feel that there is a threat of Communism in the motion-picture industry?

WD: Yes, there is, and there are many reasons why they would like to take it over or get in and control it, or disrupt it, but I don't think they have gotten very far, and I think the industry is made up of good Americans, just like in my plant, good, solid Americans.

My boys have been fighting it longer than I have. They are trying to get out from under it and they will in time if we can just show them up.

HAS: There are presently pending before this committee two bills relative to outlawing the Communist Party. What thoughts have you as to whether or not those bills should be passed?

WD: Well, I don't know as I qualify to speak on that. I feel if the thing can be proven un-American that it ought to be outlawed. I think in some way it should be done without interfering with the rights of the people. I think that will be done. I have that faith. Without interfering, I mean, with the good, American rights that we all have now, and we want to preserve.

HAS: Have you any suggestions to offer as to how the industry can be helped in fighting this menace?

WD: Well, I think there is a good start toward it. I know that I have been handicapped out there in fighting it, because they have been hiding behind this labor setup, they get themselves closely tied up in the labor thing, so that if you try to get rid of them they make a labor case out of it. We must keep the American labor unions clean. We have got to fight for them.

HAS: That is all of the questions I have, Mr. Chairman.

CHAIRMAN: Mr. Vail.

R. B. VAIL: No questions.

CHAIRMAN: Mr. McDowell.

J. MCDOWELL: No questions.

WD: Sir?

JM: I have no questions. You have been a good witness.

WD: Thank you.

CHAIRMAN: Mr. Disney, you are the fourth producer we have had as a witness, and each one of those four producers said, generally speaking, the same thing, and that is that the Communists have made inroads, have attempted inroads. I just want to point that out because there seems to be a very strong unanimity among the producers that have testified before us. In addition to producers, we have had actors and writers testify to the same. There is no doubt but what the movies are probably the greatest medium for entertainment in the United States and in the world. I think you, as a creator of entertainment, probably are one of the greatest examples in the profession. I want to congratulate you on the form of entertainment which you have given the American people and given the world and congratulate you for taking time out to come here and testify before this committee. He has been very helpful.

Do you have any more questions, Mr. Stripling?

HAS: I am sure he does not have any more, Mr. Chairman.

RES: No; I have no more questions.

CHAIRMAN: Thank you very much, Mr. Disney.

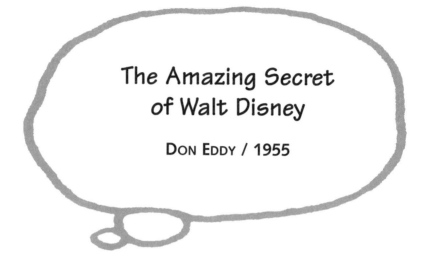

The Amazing Secret of Walt Disney

DON EDDY / 1955

From *The American Magazine*, vol. 160,
no. 2, August 1955, pp. 29, 110–15.

Walt Disney, Hollywood's world-famous creator of animated cartoon
characters and innumerable other rib-tickling, off-beat entertainments,
is riding the tallest wave of popularity and prosperity in his remarkable
career. The first movie man to make the daring plunge into television, he
has captivated the heart of America with his Davy Crockett series, and
has pulled our youngsters out of their space suits and into coon-skin
caps almost overnight.

The wistfully canine heroine of his latest film, *Lady and the Tramp*,
is already another bewitching star in the Disney firmament, along with
Snow White, Cinderella, and Captain Nemo of the *Nautilus*. And just last
month Disney turned his restless energies to something not even he had
tried before: He opened a unique project called "Disneyland"—the
nation's most fabulous amusement park. Included in its 160 incredible

acres of fun and fantasy at Anaheim, on the outskirts of Los Angeles, is a startling new Disney contribution to motion pictures—a "movie in the round," called Circarama—in which the audience is completely surrounded by a 360-degree screen.

With millions of people all over the world, I've long shared a burning curiosity about the man behind the host of beasts and beings which have won him fame and fortune. For thirty years, since the name Disney first emerged from obscurity, I have followed his achievements, from *Mickey Mouse* and *The Three Little Pigs* through *Donald Duck*, *Snow White and the Seven Dwarfs*, *Fantasia*, *Alice in Wonderland*, *Peter Pan*, and all the rest. These creations were all vividly real to me, but I knew less than nothing about their creator.

So I went, not long ago, to Burbank, California, hoping to learn the answer to one question: What amazing magical secret does Disney use to make his own dreams, and yours and mine, come true? I imagined he must have a plan or formula or recipe that any of us could use in our humdrum, everyday affairs. But I was completely unprepared for what I found. . . .

The first time I saw Walt Disney he was waiting stoically in line in his small, crowded studio cafeteria, sandwiched between typists and stagehands. He looked no different from the man next door—age fifty-four, average height, average weight, amiable, needing a haircut, his clipped mustache almost invisible against sun-toasted skin, his regulation Hollywood uniform of slacks and sports shirt as casual as though they had been the first things at hand when he got up that morning.

I watched him inch along as the line progressed, take his tray and silverware from the stacks, thoughtfully select a luncheon of orange juice, fruit salad, and chile con carne, wait while the cashier totaled his check—and pay it! I never before saw a movie producer pay for his luncheon in his own restaurant.

He carried his loaded tray through the noisy crowd to an unoccupied table, arranged his dishes on the bare boards, stacked his tray on a vacant chair, and signaled the waitress to bring coffee. He had to signal three times; the waitress nodded understandingly each time, but went on with what she was doing. In moviedom, where top producers often have their private dining rooms, I never before saw anything like that. . . .

I met Walt Disney that noontime, liked him instantly, and stretched the association over a considerable period, during which I came to know quite a bit about him. I watched him in story conferences and business meetings, accompanied him as he "fooled around" the lot—his favorite phrase and favorite pastime.

In relaxing moments, I enthused over countless snapshots he had taken of his pride and joy, his infant grandson, Chris, and noted that most of the pictures were no better than Junior makes with his toy camera. I talked with dozens of his studio associates, visited his home in Holmby Hills, was entertained informally by his lovely and understanding wife, Lillian—who once worked for him at $15 a week—and romped with their rambunctious miniature poodle, a flower-sniffing imp named Lady. Gradually, my impression of this remarkable man began to come clear.

Disney has inspired more legends, I imagine, than any living figure in the broad world of entertainment. His name is a household word in almost every civilized land. Nearly everyone has heard him called a genius—a word he dislikes, he told me, because "it is a lazy way of saying a man enjoys his work."

The commonest misconception about Disney, I believe, is that he is a sentimental softy. He isn't. He is sentimental, true enough, and to strangers he often seems soft, benign, bashful, or bewildered. Perhaps for flashing moments he is, but he never loses command of any situation. He knows what he's doing every instant. And behind the shy façade is a tough realist who can and does fight like a wildcat when the occasion demands it, and a will as inflexible as oak. When he planned to produce *Snow White* as the first full-length cartoon feature in movie history, his rivals and his bankers promptly named the project "Disney's Folly." But he went ahead and made it, anyway. One of his long-time associates, fishing for a phrase to describe him, told me he was "steel springs inside a silk pillow," and that sums it up very neatly.

He is a dreamer, but he is also an intensely earnest driver and a tireless doer, an unbending perfectionist who tolerates no compromises with himself or with any other person or thing. He knows exactly what he wants, and will work himself and his colleagues to the bone to get it. As a small example, in preparing to film the story of Pinocchio, he had a mental image of the character. He tried to describe it to his artisans. They labored valiantly but had to make 175 boy-sized dolls before catching the ineffably appealing quality Disney—but no one else— could see. His painstaking exactness sometimes drives his aides to distraction.

Although his feature films are usually loaded with emotion, although Evil is invariably vanquished and Good is triumphant, there is nothing wishy-washy, nothing holier-than-thou about their maker. He has what the military terms "command quality"—incisiveness in thought and speech, often blunt, sure and quick in his movements, a patient listener but opinionated to the point of stubbornness when his mind is made up. He is religious, but not a churchgoer, sentimental but never mawkish; a man's man, definitely not ethereal.

He has no time for small chitchat. I never heard him crack a joke or tell a funny story, much less an off-color story, and I doubt that he would listen to one. He is one of the world's greatest gamblers, plunging millions into movie ventures, yet he never bets a dime for fun. A friend recently wheedled him into flying to Las Vegas, Nevada, for an overnight holiday. Disney was bewildered by the glitter and confusion of the casinos and dumfounded by the crowds around the gambling tables. Describing it to me in his native nasal Midwestern twang, he marveled, "Why on earth do they do it, when they know they can't win?"

His dominant trait is impatience—impatience with himself, with co-workers who fail to deliver what he wants when he wants it, and with a cruel fate which perversely prevents tomorrow's chores from being finished yesterday—and this may be one of the secrets of his success.

He tries to conceal his impatience under a pose of cheerfulness, and usually succeeds in an absent-minded sort of way, but he is rarely ecstatic, occasionally morose, and often grumpy without realizing it or intending to be. The only time I heard him laugh unrestrainedly was when Mrs. Disney told him of something his grandson had done. Contrariwise, a familiar wisecrack among his 1,200 studio employees is, "Who's the boss today?" Sometimes the answer is, "It's the one with the harp and halo," but it is more apt to be, "Look out! He's wearing the wounded-tiger suit!"

His grumpiness, however, inspires little actual fear. His associates know that no matter what the provocation, Disney almost never explodes against an underling or fires a man who is honestly trying to deliver a job. Few workers who become established at the Disney studio ever leave, voluntarily or otherwise, and many have been on the payroll all their working lives. The special-effects wizard, with the improbable Disneyish name of Ubbe Iwerks (it's Dutch) has been there since the first Mickey Mouse cartoon, and two Iwerks sons are now Disneyites. Few of the top hands are women—Disney doesn't like to trust women with responsibilities—but most of them idolize the boss and call him "Walt" to his face.

He is easiest and most natural, I noticed, with manual workers—electricians, carpenters, grips, property men—and knows scores of them by their first names. In the entire plant, top to bottom, first to last, I never caught even a hint of caste consciousness, and that's rare in moviedom.

The doors of Disney's private offices have never been closed within the memory of any person with whom I talked. There are four rooms in his suite, which is on the third floor of the three-story administration building near the center of the Burbank lot on Alameda Avenue. One room is devoted to miniatures of every conceivable kind, shelves and tables crowded with them, each variety neatly grouped. They range from mantelpiece stagecoaches and trains—trains are Disney's passion—down to beer steins no wider than a match stick. There are tens of thousands of them, tiny objects he has collected personally or received from admirers all over the world.

When wrestling with a studio problem, Disney sometimes spends hours in this pint-sized museum, absently studying and rearranging the small curios, or using them to furnish doll-sized card-board houses.

A second office accommodates a serene and competent silver-haired secretary and a nimble-fingered young typist. One of the secretary's chores is to keep coffee hot and orange juice cold at all times. She also presides over a small but professionally equipped and stocked soda fountain which can instantly produce anything from a lemonade to a banana split. Disney himself is an expert soda-jerk. He has a full-sized soda fountain in a rumpus room over the garage at his home, and when his two daughters were smaller, got a large charge out of presiding at their parties.

A third room of the suite doubtless started as a business office. It has a desk and a piano. But over the years these utilitarian furnishings have become almost hidden under personal treasures and keepsakes—carved figurines, exotic native dolls, books, theater programs, hand-worked trinkets in silver and gold, and plaques and framed citations from every civilized nation on earth. Everywhere you look there are photographs of Mrs. Disney and the daughters, Diane, now Mrs. Ron Miller of Monterey, and Sharon, a student at the University of Arizona. Before some of the photographs, and elsewhere around the room, are vases of flowers.

The fourth room, where Disney spends most of his office time, is completely unbusinesslike, furnished with divans and lounging chairs in gay colors, centered with a big coffee table which serves as a desk, and flanked on one side by the soda fountain with its soft pastel lights. Sunshine streams through casement windows, touching more flowers, more photographs, more keepsakes. The mood is artistic, relaxed, and gracious.

Comfortable as these quarters are, Disney spends few of his working hours in them. He prowls constantly about the studio, popping in and out of offices and shops; listening, making suggestions, talking with any worker who seems to be engaged in an unusual job, asking innumerable questions. He wants to know how everything works, down to the most technical detail, and he becomes completely rapt in these discussions. One day I stood by almost an hour while he studied a gigantic animated crocodile intended for the Disneyland amusement park. When power was applied, the great beast crept forward and opened its gaping jaws. Fascinated by it, studying it with utter absorption, Disney, himself, crouched, crept, and gaped in rhythm to the monster's movements.

Because of these wanderings and discussions, Disney is habitually late for appointments. The office boys have standing orders to keep him in view, so that he can be located and dragged away when he has an important date. Also, from these patrols, and from his intuitiveness, which you could almost call psychic and the only psychic thing about him, he keeps intimately posted on the smallest happenings in his domain. Perhaps for that reason, the Disney plant is almost free from that common Hollywood malady called "office politics." Attesting to this is the fact that, unlike many movie moguls, Disney has no "kitchen cabinet," no sycophants, no coterie of favorites. Except for his brother Roy, who manages the Disney enterprises, he walks alone, essentially and congenitally a lonely man.

He has no interest in night clubs or café society, likes the theater but hates to leave home in the evenings, and moves socially in a very small circle of friends, most of them cultivated by Mrs. Disney. A lovely, warmly gracious woman, completely down to earth, Lilly Disney makes no secret of the hard times the family weathered in early years, shakes her head in wondering amusement at some of Walt's idiosyncrasies, but seldom tries to interfere with him. She is perhaps the only individual who thoroughly understands him.

Mrs. Disney has long since become inured to her husband's devotion to his work, which she calls "my rival." One day she remarked, with a twinkle, "If it ever comes to a showdown between his studio and his wife, Heaven help me!" Such a showdown is not likely; the Disneys have a tender rapport, an intimate companionship which is only strained, and then momentarily, when Lilly wants to step out socially and Walt balks.

For recreation, Disney works with his hands. He made a scale-model steam-powered train which operates on a half-mile of tracks and sidings on the grounds of his home, through a tunnel and over trestles. Even adults can ride it, sitting on the tops of boxcars. For a long time he loved it passionately and ran it at every opportunity, but it hasn't turned a wheel now for almost a year—ever since he became enthralled with building a bigger train to run through Disneyland.

His home hobby now is a red barn he built down a slope from his home—a workshop fitted with small precision power tools and hundreds of hand tools. When he has problems on his mind, he goes to the barn after dinner in the evenings and makes miniatures—not baubles, but toy trolleys, horses and wagons, little people, tiny towns, and doll-sized furniture. Most of these things have the unmistakable Disney quirkiness.

Of the barn itself, Walt told me, "It's an exact duplicate of my dad's barn on the old farm at Marceline, Missouri; I remembered every detail of it." Inside, he showed me his tools, the power machines tidily covered against dust and moisture, and his current project, an old-fashioned bar-bershop about eighteen inches square in which the barber chair will pivot and recline, the solid brass cuspidors can be moved around, mirrors are painted with prices (haircuts: 25 cents), and infinitely tiny shaving brushes stand in rows of miniscule mugs, each ornately painted with the name of its imaginary owner.

A rumpled blanket under one of the workbenches will never be moved. It was the resting place of a devoted old dog, Dee-Dee, which until her death, not long ago, shared these nocturnal vigils with Disney.

"I used to go out in the kitchen after dinner," Walt remembered, his voice throaty, "and cram my pockets with bologna and stuff for Dee-Dee, and we'd come down here and fool around. That dog was so darned smart you wouldn't believe it. She'd get up off the blanket exactly at midnight, stretch herself, and then start deviling me to go up to bed. She wouldn't let up."

Now, not infrequently, Mrs. Disney has to go down in the small hours and coax her husband to call it a night.

The baby grandson, Christopher Disney Miller, whose father, now in the Army, was an outstanding University of Southern California football star, is the apple of Walt's eye. "He's the first man I ever had in the family," he says with unconcealed pride. "You know, I've been henpecked by my womenfolks all my life." Nobody, incidentally, including Walt, believes this; it's a family joke.

Although he insists he will never try to influence young Chris, because "grandparents should keep out of it; anyhow kids have to be themselves, find their own way," I noticed he already has a fancy pony saddle cached away, and he enlarged the tiny tots' section of Disneyland the day after the baby was born. One day, showing me a motorized kiddie ride he was building in the park, he chuckled jubilantly, "Won't Chris get a bang out of that!"

I doubt that Disney is aware of the ramifications of his own nature. He seems to think of himself as a hard-headed, hard-working, hard-pressed citizen carrying a world of worry on his shoulders, bowed down with responsibilities. He thinks he has been lucky up to now, but that the whole thing could explode at any moment. That realistically pessimistic streak, not uncommon among artists, keeps him humble, grateful to the world that has been good to him, completely devoid of snobbishness or pretension, and gives him an earthy kinship with humanity which could explain, at least in part, the universal appeal of his pictures.

Another explanation could be his early environment: He came up the hard way. His parents were Elias Disney, an Irish-Canadian, and Flora Call Disney, of German-American descent. Elias Disney was a stiff-backed Socialist, almost fanatically religious, an old-fashioned family martinet who imposed such severe discipline on his children that the two oldest boys, Herbert, now sixty-six, and Raymond, sixty-four, left home when very young. Herbert spent his life as a Los Angeles mail carrier, retiring recently. Raymond is an insurance broker at Burbank, California, with an office near the studio, and handles much of the company's business.

Roy, the third son, was eight years old when Walt was born at Chicago, Illinois, December 5, 1901, followed in two years by the family's only girl, now Mrs. Ruth Disney Beecher, of Portland, Oregon. Roy's job was to keep an eye on little Walt, and between these two boys grew a camaraderie which has endured. They sometimes argue, but never seriously; neither can remember an unkind word. Roy is president of the Disney empire and reputed to be the financial brain. He and Walt make a formidable team.

The Disneys moved from Chicago to the Missouri farm and then to Kansas City, where Walt delivered newspapers, competed in amateur vaudeville, took sidewalk photos, carried mail in the Christmas rush, and was struggling through high school when World War I erupted. Only sixteen, turned down for military service, he was hired as a chauffeur and sent overseas by the Red Cross, where he was bawled out for painting cartoons on his ambulance. Today, if it could be found, that vehicle would be priceless.

Unwilling to return to school after the war, young Disney worked briefly as a $50-a-month hack artist for a farm journal before teaming with Ubbe Iwerks, also an aspiring teen-aged artist, in a free-lance commercial art studio. Their earnings didn't pay the rent, so Walt landed a job with a movie theatrical slide company at $35 a week.

The break which shaped his life came when he worked out his own system for animating cartoons. "I didn't invent it," Walt insists; "I got it out of a reference book at the library." He made a sample advertising reel for a theater owner and of this momentous event Disney remembers:

"I was sitting behind him in the theater, just the two of us. I was nervous as a cat, wondering what he would think of it, and when he whirled around and snapped, 'I like it. Is it expensive?' I blurted quickly, 'No sir; I can make it for thirty cents a foot.' He said, 'It's a deal; I'll buy all you can make.' I went out walking on air, and it must have been an hour before I realized I had forgotten one small detail—the profit. Thirty cents a foot was exactly what it cost me to make it."

Then as now, money is something Walt understands only vaguely, and thinks about only when he doesn't have enough to finance his current enthusiasm, whatever it may be.

Destined to popularize an entirely new type of entertainment, the Disney cartoon system, improved and refined countless times and now covered by a thick blanket of patents, was the foundation of the Disney enterprises. From it have grown a score of feature-length cartoon spec-tacles, all with sound and color, plus hundreds of short subjects. Together, they represent about $50,000,000—money which they have earned, and which has been immediately reinvested.

A widely credited myth has it that Mickey Mouse was inspired by a real live mouse which lived in Disney's attic studio when he was a starv-ing young artist. The story is apocryphal. There was never such a mouse nor such an attic studio. Mickey was an invention of necessity, dreamed up out of thin air on a railroad train carrying despondent young Walt Disney and his bride to California from New York after a crushing, disillu-sioning defeat in his first hand-to-hand encounter with Big Business.

He had reached Hollywood first in 1923 with one suit, one sweater, one shoe box of drawing tools, and four $10 bills. Roy had preceded him and saved $250. He and Walt formed a partnership—with Roy's money—and borrowed $500 from an Uncle Robert, who let them share his spare bedroom. They rented part of a real-estate office, made a down payment on a used movie camera, hired two girls—one of them Lillian Bounds, a tourist from Lewiston, Idaho—and began making sample cartoons. A New York film buyer ordered from them a series called *Oswald the Rabbit*. They were in business.

Flushed with success, Walt married Miss Bounds, sent to Kansas City for his old partner, Iwerks, hired about twenty other artists, and "went Hollywood" for the first and only time in his life by buying an ostentatious Moon automobile. He was riding high when suddenly he heard that his buyer was making other arrangements for *Oswald*, and that most of the artists he had trained, trusted, and praised were preparing to desert him en masse. Refusing to believe it, he hurried to New York, taking his bride for a belated honeymoon. The rumors proved true. All his dreams came tumbling down around his ears.

"He was like a raging lion on the train coming home," Mrs. Disney told me. "He had gambled everything we had—which wasn't much, but seemed a lot to us—on the *Oswald* series. All he could say, over and over, was that he'd never work for anyone again as long as he lived: he'd be his own boss. I didn't share his long-range viewpoint. I was in a state of shock, scared to death."

Clattering out of Chicago, Walt seized a handful of railroad stationery and roughed out a scenario for a cartoon to be called *Plane Crazy*. (Lindbergh's flight had just electrified the world.) Its star was to be a mouse—why a mouse, not even Disney can now recall—and its name was to be Mortimer.

"He read the script to me," Mrs. Disney remembers, "but I couldn't focus on it: I was too upset. The only thing that got through to me was that horrible name, Mortimer—horrible for a mouse, at least—and I'm afraid I made quite a scene about it. When I blew up, Walt calmed down. After a while he asked quietly, 'What would you think of Mickey—Mickey Mouse?' I said it sounded better than Mortimer, and that's how Mickey was born."

There was a long lean spell before Disney's confidence in Mickey paid off. Walt had to sacrifice his flashy Moon for $425 to meet the payroll, and Lilly had to introduce the later-popular bare-legged fad because she snagged her last pair of silk stockings on rough board stairs leading to a cluttered garage which was their studio. But when sound came in, and Mickey acquired a voice (Walt's own, in falsetto), the Mouse suddenly soared to heights of popularity, siring the long line of Disney characters which everyone knows.

Mickey was an instantaneous idea born of an emergency, but Disney's ideas seldom come in blinding flashes; they usually result from his avid curiosity. One of his present smash hits, for example, is the outdoor series which includes *Seal Island*, *Beaver Valley*, *Nature's Half Acre*, and others. It grew out of his life-long interest in animals, but it was sparked accidentally when a photographing couple asked him to look at films they had made in the Arctic. He was not particularly impressed with these pictures, but he was fascinated by their intimate knowledge of wildlife. He commissioned them to make other subjects they had in mind, and they are still at it—as are some eighteen other camera-technical crews Disney has presently scattered in tropical jungles, on deserts, oceans, and mountaintops all around the world.

Almost unconsciously, he adapts nature's laws to human affairs. One day we were discussing deadlines—whether an individual works best under pressure, as he has done so often. Disney said he thought everyone needed deadlines. "Even the beavers. They loaf around all summer, but when they are faced with the winter deadline, they work like fury. If we didn't have deadlines, we'd stagnate."

Disney's confidence has inspired countless true stories, but none is more typical than the case of the pleasure park, Disneyland. Personally, I never saw anything like that park, built among old orange groves clear across the city from Hollywood. From the outside it resembles the turreted castle of a fairy prince. Inside, it has everything conceivable from a flea circus to a turbid jungle river complete with realistic cannibals, crocodiles, hippopotamuses, and with gorillas which snarl, scream, and charge at customers on a full-sized steamboat. Brother Roy told me how it happened:

"I think it started with his toy trains; he always wanted to build a big play-train for the public. For years, too, he has been talking about some kind of park where people could enjoy all these creations he dreams up. It sounded crazy. We were in the movie business, not the amusement-park business. We didn't know a thing in the world about amusement parks. None of us around Walt wanted any part of his amusement park. His banker used to hide under the desk when Walt started talking about that park. But you couldn't stop him. He was confident it would be wonderful.

"The first I knew, more than a year ago, he had artists drawing sketches and blueprints. I wondered where the money was coming from, but I didn't ask; it was his baby, and he could have it. The next I heard, he had hocked his life insurance. Still I kept quiet. Finally, one day, Walt's banker called up and said Walt had been in to see him. 'It's about that park,' the banker said. 'We went over the plans. You know, Roy, that park is a wonderful idea!' I nearly fell out of my chair. I asked whether Walt had tried to borrow money. The banker said, 'Yes sir, he did. And you know what? I loaned it to him!'"

Walt had invested $250,000 of his own money, practically all borrowed on insurance and personal notes, before his associates were able to see what he had in mind. Then, like the banker, they came down with explosive enthusiasm. Proper financing was arranged and the job roared ahead. Originally estimated to cost some $3,500,000, the most recent budget was for $17,000,000, and nobody knows where it will end. Walt told me, his eyes sparkling, "It will *never* be finished!" if you ask me, I think he is building it mostly for young Chris Miller.

Walt's courage is best typified, I think, by his experience with television. As nearly everyone knows, television was long a dirty word in the ears of Hollywood's movie moguts, who believed it hurts theater attendance. Not even the boldest of them could be persuaded that a feature picture shown first on TV would earn a three-dollar bill at theaters. Of all producers, only Disney believed otherwise. "He said television was essentially a good thing," one of his colleagues told me, "and that we should encourage it. He believed black-and-white television would serve as an advertising medium, and that people who saw tantalizing portions of a good picture on TV would later go to the theaters to see the whole thing in color on the big screen. I didn't agree with him, and I don't know anyone in show business who did. It was a tremendous gamble, and it took superb courage to try it out."

Disney tried it first with Davy Crockett, then with some of his best nature films, finally with segments of his multimillion-dollar feature *Lady and the Tramp*. He ran them several times. Experts figure they were seen by 50,000,000 TV viewers before being released for theater showings. And what happened?

As this is written, it appears that Disney, the maker of dreams, has once more out-foxed and confounded the worldly Hollywood wiseacres, completely reversing their concepts of intelligent theatrical procedure. For the same films, except for color and big screen, are playing to stand-out audiences in all their early showings. It is entirely possible that his pioneering may pave the way for TV premieres of brand-new feature films, either prior to or concurrently with their theater debuts. Millions of us will agree that this would be a welcome relief from the antediluvian movie horrors now composing much of the TV fare.

Disney's constancy to his convictions has never been more forcefully demonstrated than when he has been criticized for scenes which, some mothers said, their children shouldn't be shown—not on a basis of morality, but because they tended to be overexciting. An early example was *The Skeleton Dance*, a ghoulish-gay *Silly Symphony*, and others have been the witches, ogres, giants, and dragons in several features. In each case, Disney stood pat. He tried to tell me why.

"I don't believe in playing down to children. I didn't treat my youngsters like fragile flowers, and I think no parent should. Children are people, and they should have to reach to learn about things, to understand things, just as adults have to reach if they want to grow in mental stature. Life is composed of lights and shadows, and we would be untruthful, insincere, and saccharine if we tried to pretend there were no shadows. Most things are good, and they are the strongest things, but there are evil things, too, and you do a child no favor by trying to shield it from reality. The important thing is to teach a child that Good always triumphs over Evil, and that is what our pictures do."

The severest storm centered around a wildlife scene showing the birth of a buffalo calf. Protests cascaded in from all around the nation, but Disney refused to eliminate the scene. "Aren't we getting prudish," he demanded tartly, "when we say natural processes are objectionable? I want my children to know about these things, and to learn them from nature; they are part of existence, as natural and unashamed as breathing." The scenes were shown in many cities, eliminated in others. In neither event did Disney take a hand.

Much as his fiddle-playing father and choir-singing mother had done to their brood, except with much more gentleness and companionship, Disney reared his own daughters to be self-effacing and enjoy simplicity. One of his fetishes, enthusiastically seconded by understanding Mrs. Disney, was to keep them unaware that their daddy was something of a big wheel. Few studio people were invited to the house, the Disneys never talked shop before their children, and the girls secretly were rather ashamed that their father did something with silly little movie cartoons. Walt never knew this until one day, rushing home from an afternoon party, Diane threw herself into his arms, embraced him wildly, and screamed hysterically, "Father, are you *the* Walt Disney?" But it was a long time before they ceased regretting that he didn't make pictures with such heroes as Clark Gable and Spencer Tracy.

As the girls grew older, their spending allowances were kept small, their wardrobes limited, and their extravagances discouraged. In 1952, however, in an unprecedented splurge, Walt took five women to Europe—Mrs. Disney, the daughters, a niece, and a friend of Diane's. On this trip he taught them to "reach" for what they wanted.

"Before we started," Mrs. Disney reports, "this poor henpecked character laid down the law, but good! He told the girls he intended to have a good time for himself, didn't want to be disturbed by silly females, and was not to be teased to do anything he didn't want to do. Well, you know how long that lasted! But it seems he really meant it."

In New York, the girls begged him to take them to Washington, D.C. He flatly refused. "If you want to go," he said when they besieged him in their hotel suite, "go ahead. But I'm not going with you." They asked when and how they might go. "Suit yourself," he said testily. "You're old enough to think for yourselves. Go down and ask the porter; he'll tell you about trains."

Wide-eyed and nervous, never having traveled alone, the girls trooped down-stairs. "And you know what their father did?" Mrs. Disney demanded with a smile. "The minute they left the room, he called the porter and told him exactly what he wanted done. Then he called the hotel in Washington and gave explicit instructions. The girls had a whirl for themselves, of course, and they'll never know until they read this that their father arranged the whole thing."

In Europe, he followed much the same procedure.

On the surface, it would appear that Disney has reached the pinnacle of success and fame. What worlds are left for him to conquer? But then I remembered—they have been saying that about him ever since Mickey Mouse first took the world by storm, and *Snow White* brought in its first $10,000,000. And somehow you can't believe there are any heights that can't be scaled by a man who knows the secret of making dreams come true.

This special secret, it seems to me, can be summarized in four C's. They are Curiosity, Confidence, Courage, and Constancy, and the greatest of these is Confidence. Without his confidence, Disney would not be where he is. When he believes a thing, he believes it all over, implicitly and unquestioningly.

From his insatiable curiosity, as persistent and all-embracing as a child's, he gets his ideas. When he settles on one idea, his confidence takes supreme command; nothing can shake it. His courage keeps it alive and active against all obstacles, and he has plenty of obstacles. And he is constant to it until it becomes reality. Then he drops it abruptly and rarely mentions it again.

If it is a business venture (he follows the same procedure with his playthings) he hopes it turns out profitably. Not all of them do, but he doesn't fret about his flops. When he makes a profit, he doesn't squander it or hide it away; he immediately plows it back into a fresh project. He has little respect for money as such, regards it merely as a medium for financing new ideas, and neither wishes nor intends to amass a personal fortune.

Neither he nor brother Roy has ever drawn a dividend from their company, although they have pyramided a $500 borrowed bankroll into tangible assets in excess of $10,000,000 and, with their families, own 54 percent of the outstanding stock. When I asked Walt how he kept from worrying about profits—which I found difficult to believe—he shrugged and said, "Why worry? If you've done the very best you can, worrying won't make it any better. Anyhow, I've noticed that most things in life even up in the long run." He worries about many things, but not about water over the dam. I wish I could do likewise!

One night down in the barn workshop I told him my theory of the four C's, and then asked him point-blank if he knew the secret of his own success, and if he could tell me and others like me how to make our dreams come true, as he had done.

"Why, sure," he growled, glancing up from a lathe where he was shaving threadlike curls from a brass rod. "You do it by working. Working, just like I've always done. Why, man"—and his voice changed from a growl to a rising note of enthusiasm—"I'm fooling around with a couple of ideas—Here, sit down. Let me tell you about them."

I was still sitting there, hypnotized, enthralled, when Lilly called him to come up to bed.

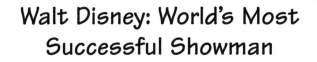

Walt Disney: World's Most Successful Showman

PAUL MOLLOY / 1957

From *Success Unlimited IV*,
September 1957, pp. 4–7, 26.

Walt Disney is an easy man to get to, but he's a little hard to find.

I found him in a luxurious office in the heart of his multimillion-dollar studios in Burbank, California. To reach him, you have to sort of tread nimbly through a countless array of awards, plaques, cups, medals, trophies and testimonials—each a monument to some "Disney's Folly."

Mischief twinkled in his eyes as he leaned back in his chair amid this cornucopia of universal acclaim. The man with the ageless heart of Peter Pan was trying to laugh off his seemingly unlimited success. "I guess," he said, "I'm just corny through and through."

I guess he's right. Certainly there is corn in his favorite maxim: "You don't know what you can do unless you try."

Everybody knows that. But Disney saw it as more than just a pious adage. He put it to work. The way to success, he said, was obvious:

"Quit talking—and start doing it."

In earlier years, when Disney would quit talking and start doing it, friends, relatives and associates—and especially his creditors—were regularly horrified by his distressing lack of what they called "common sense."

Today at fifty-six, Disney looks back on a harvest of corn that has made him the world's most successful showman, and muses: "Sometimes I wonder if common sense isn't another way of saying fear.

"And fear too often spells failure."

We strolled into the studio restaurant, Disney's restaurant, and I wondered if he thought back on those Kansas City days when he lived on bread and beans.

He was nineteen then—brave, bright and broke. He had convinced a few backers he could turn out animated cartoons, a revolutionary form of entertainment, and they had put up $15,000. Frantically he turned out a crude, jerky version of *Puss in Boots*. It was promptly rejected everywhere, and Disney's backer pussyfooted away.

Now he sat in his "office," an untidy room above a shoemaker's shop, with a can of beans and a loaf of bread. The telephone rang. It was from the head of a dental institute who had asked Disney to do a cartoon illustrating the care of teeth.

"Come on over and let's set the deal," his caller said.

"I can't," Disney replied.

"Why not?"

"I haven't any shoes. They were falling apart and I left them downstairs at the shoemaker's. He won't let me have them until I dig up a dollar and a half."

The dentist hustled over with money and Disney handled the job, doubtless convinced that:

"Fear too often spells failure."

It could have spelled failure many times because his daughter, Diane, recalls: "I can think of ten or twenty crises in my father's life."

It could have spelled failure in his formative years in Marceline, Missouri, where his father operated a farm that was running the family into debt. When the Disneys moved to Kansas City, Disney immediately took a paper route, an early morning chore he handled for six years.

At fourteen he talked his father into allowing him to take art classes on Saturday afternoons, while the other youngsters were doing what youngsters do on Saturday afternoons. At fifteen, he was aboard the Santa Fe, hawking oranges and magazines, to pay for the art course—for the man who was to become respected and imitated the world over halted his formal education in the first year of high school.

After World War I (too young to fight, he served as an ambulance driver with the American Red Cross) Disney returned to Kansas City where he hired on with a film advertising company at $40 a week. It was then he decided to begin animation experiments. He had no space, no equipment—only a sense of direction.

"Fear too often spells failure."

Disney trotted off to a friend, talked glibly and borrowed a movie camera. Then he went to his boss, talked glibly, and borrowed his garage. What came of this was the $15,000 *Puss in Boots* disaster.

He had saved enough to buy his own movie camera and now decided on a blockbuster: Why not introduce human beings into film featuring cartoon characters?

With characteristic industry Disney produced a series called *Alice in Cartoonland*. It was shown to distributors in New York. It spawned some interest, but nary a nibble. Now Disney was not only broke, but dangerously in debt.

If he was to crash into show business, he decided he must go to the center of show business. He boarded a train and a few days later landed in Hollywood.

This was 1923. When he arrived in the cinema capital Disney wore a threadbare pair of pants, a checkered coat (he didn't own a suit). In his imitation leather suitcase was one shirt, two pairs of socks and some drawing material. He had sold his movie camera for train fare and his fortune was exactly $40.

"Fear too often spells failure."

At twenty-one, he was looking for a director's job. He was laughed out of several studios at a time when the creation of another cartoonist, Felix the Cat, was doing well. Disney wondered if he wasn't "too late" with his original ideas.

"Fear too often spells failure."

He rented a camera, built a stand from scrap and borrowed another garage to continue his experiments. Then came proof that the creative artist must never flirt with fear.

A distributor in New York saw a now forgotten *Alice in Cartoonland* sequence and put in an order for more. In this project Disney spent three years, paying off $5 and $10 debts, and eventually struck on a new character, Oswald the Rabbit. By now competitors began to talk about this man Disney, and one actually tried to lure away his small staff.

If they were after him, Disney reasoned, he was ahead of them, throwing them neatly off the track with still a new character, a mouse he christened Mickey. Distributors were aghast; who could popularize a mouse? Said one, curtly: "It's no use, Walt. Nobody's ever heard of Mickey Mouse." The world would later hear of it because—

"Fear too often spells failure."

But when the first Mickey Mouse episode was ready for showing, misfortune intruded again. At the very moment that Mickey was to make his controversial debut, out came a motion picture called *The Jazz Singer*. Sound had come to the moving pictures.

"Fear too often spells failure."

Disney decided he would introduce sound to cartoon film. Not only did he accomplish this, on his own, but he developed the basis for the system of sound synchronization used in cartoons to this day.

The climb was to take its toll. In 1931 Disney suffered a nervous breakdown, was ordered to lay down his paints and do nothing but rest.

One year later, Disney had recovered, introduced color into his cartoons and turned out *Flowers and Trees*, the industry's first sound-and-color cartoon. It won Disney his first Oscar. He has since won twenty-four others.

The rest is history. In 1933 came *Three Little Pigs* and now the world was humming and whistling the Disney songs.

Disney sought perfection so he underwrote tuition in art courses for his staff and, to achieve accuracy in the movement of animals, became the first producer to send his cameraman into the field to film wildlife. Disney sat by the hour and the day, studying these films, observing the delicacy of a hummingbird in flight and the frenetic skitter of a squirrel darting up a tree. To this day Disney has not ceased learning. In his machine shop he asked his superintendent to teach him the handling of metal lathes and other tools. With this knowledge he constructed his own miniature train. He also served as an apprentice in his carpenter shop.

"If I had a headache," he recalled, "I'd go to that shop and it would clear up, and I'd feel fine. A man needs a new set of problems to take his mind off his old ones."

As he guided me through his immense studios, I was impressed by the man's simplicity. Wearing slacks and an open shirt he might have passed for an employee as he poked about the shops, tightening a bolt here, fingering a mold there. The man has maintained his interest in all things, including the small things.

Long-time workers hailed him by his first name as he passed. Disney turned to me and chuckled: "Anybody gets highbrow around here—out he goes!"

In its first two years, 7,500,000 persons have visited his famed Disneyland Park, perhaps the one monument Disney wants to leave behind. He is there himself, at least twice a week, to see that operations remain smooth. Besides, he loves people. Says he:

"Now, I'm a grandfather and have a good many gray hairs. But if I'm no longer young in age, I hope I stay young enough in spirit never to fear failure."

"Fear too often spells failure."

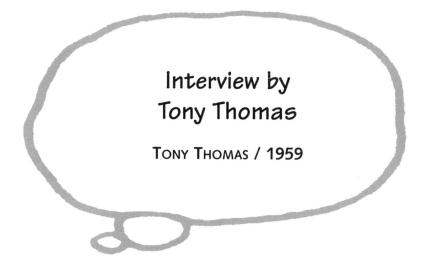

Interview by
Tony Thomas

Tony Thomas / 1959

On the audio recording, *Voices from the Hollywood Past*. From the Walt Disney Archives.

W: I came to Hollywood, and arrived here in August 1923, with $30 in my pocket and a coat and a pair of trousers that didn't match. And one half of my suitcase had my shirts and underwear and things—the other half had my drawing materials. [Laughs] It was a cardboard suitcase at that.

T: [also laughing]: We don't think of you in terms of the silent picture era. What did you do when you finally got out here?
W: Well, I tried to get a job doing anything I could in a studio, so I could learn. I was a little discouraged with the cartoon at that time—I felt at that time that I was getting into it too late. In other words, I thought the cartoon business was established in such a way that there was no chance

to break into it. So I tried to get a job in Hollywood, working in the picture business so I could learn it. I would have liked to have been a director, or any part of that. It wasn't open, so before I knew it I had my drawing board out and I started back to the cartoon. And I was able to secure a contract for twelve of these short films. And I did all the drawing myself . . . I did—I had no help at all, I was all alone. But I made the first six practically alone. Then, at that time I was able to get some of the boys that had been with me in Kansas City to come out. So then, from the seventh on, I had some help. And I got by the first year, and they were fairly successful, and that led to other things. And with some of the boys I'd worked with in Kansas City augmenting the set-up, I was able to eventually build an organization. And it reached a point that I had so many working with me, and there was so much time and attention demanded that I had to drop the drawing end of it myself. But I've never regretted it, because drawing was always a means to an end with me. And so through these other boys, who were good draftsmen and artists in many different phases of the business . . . very talented people—and coordinating their talents is what has built this business. And if I hadn't dropped the drawing end of it myself, I don't think I'd have built this organization.

T: When did you establish your own company, to deal with that, then?
W: 1923. My brother was here, and in effect, the government helped subsidize us—and I'll explain that to you. My brother was a veteran of the first World War, and he had been hospitalized and things, and so he was receiving a certain disability compensation. It amounted to about $85 a month. And we lived on that while we established the Studio. And from that time on, my brother Roy and I have been together in this business, and until the year 1940 we didn't have a stockholder.

T: When was Mickey Mouse born?
W: Mickey Mouse came about in 1928.

T: With sound, I presume.
W: Well, no. The first Mickey Mouse was made silent, and while we were making the first Mickey Mouse sound came. So we decided that there's no sense in making anything more silent, and we immediately switched to sound—and we didn't have any sound equipment or anything else, but we went ahead and made 'em for sound, and we eventually got sound on 'em—and of course it, I think, played the big part in establishing Mickey Mouse.

T: Where did the idea for Mickey come from?

W: Well, it came about through a situation that . . . I was contracting with a middleman for my films—they were being released through Universal—and he was a rather unscrupulous character, and he thought he could cut in and move in a little better. And I pulled away from him, and I was left alone, and he had a right to the character. So that was one of the big lessons I learned, and from then on I said, "There's no middle-man." He contributed nothing; we did everything. So I had to get a new character. Now, I had been doing a rabbit—it was called "Oswald the Rabbit." So I had to have a new character. And I was coming back after this meeting in New York, and Mrs. Disney was with me, and it was on the train—in those days, you know, it was three days over, three days from New York—and when I said, "We've got to get a new character," and I'd always . . . well, I'd fooled around a lot with little mice, and they were always cute characters, and they hadn't been overdone in the picture field—they'd been used, but never featured. So well, I decided it would be with a mouse, because at that time I didn't have Mickey as more or less a normal scale human being. I had him as a scaled mouse, with overscaled props. Well, that's how it came about. And then the name came: "What would you call him?"—and the euphony there of "Mickey Mouse." I had him "Mortimer" first, and my wife shook her head, and then I tried "Mickey" and she nodded the other way and that was it.

T: Is it true that you did the voice for Mickey yourself in the early days?

W [in Mickey's voice]: Oh yeah, I still do it. [They both laugh]

T: I was going to ask you if you could, and you still can [laughs].

W [still in Mickey's voice]: Well, it's just a falsetto. And we were foolin' around and tryin' to get a voice for a mouse, and we didn't know what a mouse would sound like, so I said, "It's kind of like this." And the guy said, "Well, why don't you do it?" And I knew I'd always be on the pay-roll, so [laughs] I did it.

T [laughing]: When was Donald Duck born?

W [in his own voice again]: Donald came about four or five years after Mickey Mouse, and I heard the voice on the radio. It was, well, almost an amateur program, and this boy was imitating animals and things, and birds, and he had this little gag that he ended his act with, about the lit-tle duck—he had it a girl duck—

T: A girl duck . . . ?

W: —reciting "Mary Had a Little Lamb." It was that odd voice. When I immediately got in touch with that radio station, they didn't know who he was—he'd gone. I traced him down and found he was working for a dairy. And he was doing little lectures in the schools on bird life, wearing the uniform of this dairy, advertising the milk—an indirect way of getting their advertising. And he'd move to his classrooms and tell about the birds and how the meadowlark would sound, and all of that. So he wasn't making much money, and I said, "Well, I can pay you a little more than they're payin' if you want to come over here, and we'll find out what we can do with that voice." So, he was here on the payroll for about a year before I . . . the thing that kept throwing me all the time was the girl duck. And finally I said, "Well, it don't have to be a girl—it could be a . . . a boy duck!" you know. So, we ended up with Donald.

T: What about all the other characters, like Pluto? Did you think of these yourself or was it sort of a joint—?

W: Well, they evolved. Pluto . . . we were doing a short with Mickey Mouse—I think it was called The Chain Gang—where he escaped from prison and they sent the hounds after him. And one of these hounds—we were foolin' around with this hound—it was on the trail of this runaway mouse, and out of that came this friendly hound character. And from there on we said, "Well, we can use him." And before we knew it, we had him in as Mickey's pal. Oh, we had changed him a little bit from the hound, but that's how it started. And, we'll spring out of something. Now the Donald Duck came from this voice, and we tried to find the character; then I had a little subject come up where I used a duck, and it was Donald. And from there on he blossomed out.

T: And the family grew.

W: Yeah.

T: Where are they all now?

W: Well, they're very active right now. We do an awful lot with them in television, and we do do a certain number of short features to accompany our longer features.

T: Mickey is still working then?

W: Oh, yes.

T: We're very happy to know that.
W: He's thirty years old now.

T: That's a pretty old mouse, isn't it?
W: Well, through the years he's got . . . he's a little better constructed mouse than he ever was. I think that he's—

T: He's improved with age.
W: He's improved with age, yeah.

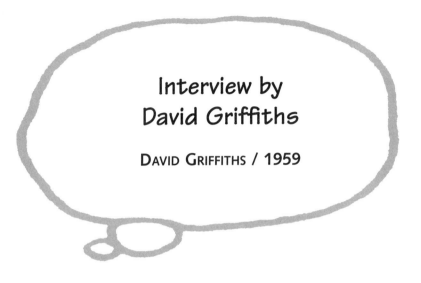

Interview by
David Griffiths

DAVID GRIFFITHS / 1959

From the Walt Disney Archives.

Q: There seem to be conflicting stories on how you originated Mickey Mouse. I should be grateful for clarification. Did you ever keep pet mice? **A:** Mickey Mouse as a cartoon character came into being as a result of my having lost the rights to Oswald the Rabbit because of a dispute with the releasing company which refused to renew the contract on what I regarded as the only feasible basis of continued production. This faced our company with a critical situation. We had to create a new character in a hurry to survive. And find a market for it. We canvassed all the animal characters we thought suitable for the movie fable fashion of the time. All the good ones—the ones that would have instant appeal and would be comparatively easy to draw—seemed to have been preempted by the other companies in the cartoon animation field. Finally a mouse was suggested, debated and put on the drawing boards as the best bet.

That was Mickey, so named at Mrs. Disney's suggestion. After his first public appearance in New York in *Steamboat Willie* he was on his now well-known way to making movie history and setting a new entertainment vogue.

About keeping a pet mouse: yes, I had [a pet mouse] during my grade school days in Kansas City. He was a gentle little field mouse. I kept him in my pocket on a string leash. Whenever things seemed to get a bit dull between classes, I would let him rove about on his leash under the seats to get laughs from the other kids. And he got laughs—until the teacher rather sharply disagreed with my sense of extracurricular activities and made me keep the little beastie at home.

Perhaps it was the fond memory of him—and of others of his clan who used to pick up lunch crumbs in our first cartoon studio, the family garage, that came to mind when we needed so desperately to find a new character to survive. . . . Mickey Mouse's country forefathers, you might say.

Q: There has been occasional criticism about the amount of horrific material sometimes included in your films. I note that one of your first films, *Skeleton Dance*, was denounced as "too gruesome," and the witch in *Snow White* was said to have frightened many children. Was there some good reason for the inclusion of such material in films seen by children?

A: This is an old topic of occasional critical inquiry—this curious reference to "horrific material" included in our presentation of the classic fairytales.

All the world's great fairytales, it must be remembered, are essentially morality tales, opposing good and bad, virtue and villainy, in dramatic terms easily understood and approved by children. Without such clash of good and evil and the prevalence of goodness—of the good people—fairytales like *Snow White, Cinderella, Pinocchio, Sleeping Beauty* long since would have died because they would have had no meaning. Now if you're going to give goodness something really important to fight for, to conquer—something children as well as elders can root for and identify themselves with—you've got to make villainy a worthy foe. Out of this need the world's fairytale literature has created its witches, its evil fairies, its hags, its "bad people." Of course they are repellent; they have to be. But in our movie versions of these venerable morality plays—read to youngsters by parents of many, many generations over several centuries—we have tried to keep all the elements in proper balance of entertainment. We have often eliminated or greatly modified the "horrific" material in the classic fairytale literature. Psychologists concerned with motion picture entertainment have long poo-poohed the occasional fear of parents that children are harmfully affected by the theatrical clash of good and evil, so long as the hero triumphs without too much peril to himself. What relief and glee there is then! On this point the consensus of exhibitors the world over coincides with our own experience in almost forty years of showmanship. We don't pussyfoot with evil; we deal with it forthrightly.

Most critics and commentators of our product understand this. The great mass of our adult family members also understand it well.

Q: Has your work ever been consciously directed toward combating cruelty to animals? Many children must have grown up with a kindlier feeling toward animals as a result of seeing your films.
A: We have not *consciously* or *deliberately* directed our nature pictures and wild animal dramas toward combating cruel human treatment. That they have had such an effect we have often been told. And this has gratified all of us who share this work on the True-Life Adventures, in the field and in the studio. Our aim in these pictures is to present animal nature honestly, in all its phases of comedy and sometimes tragedy, its family life, training of the young, heroic defense of the helpless and the elemental emotions which govern their existence as our fellow creatures on this earth. So presented, they tug at our sympathies and understanding and therefore more humane regard. I am sure that children all over the world—and their parents as well—have a kindlier attitude toward wild creatures after having seen them in our True-Life Adventures. . . . I'm sure even mice have had it easier as a result of Mickey's antics.

Q: How many employees are there at your studio? And is this the highest number you have ever had?
A: Our present roster shows 1500 employees at the studio, with 100 to 200 plus or minus as the production needs fluctuate from week to week. This is the high mark. In 1940, for comparison, we had around 1200 to 1300. The present mark indicates our production expansion in the past few years, with increases in every department.

Q: Have you ever taken heed of commentary to the effect that some of your nature pictures are rather too coy and that several of your [cartoon] heroines' voices have been rather harsh?

A: We have our own approach to wildlife nature as entertainment. We are not telling the dry academic natural history of bird and beast and reptile in these dramas seen from the animals' standpoint. Our narration is governed in its text and delivery to this presentation of wild animal life stories observed and photographed in the natural state. That the narration expressed a sympathetic and "all knowing" human attitude toward the animal kingdom—not the zoological detached reaction—may have seemed to some critics and commentators as "coy." This is an opinion based on the commentator's attitude toward nature. It bespeaks a viewpoint. Ours corresponds to that of the best current nature writers and is based on what our naturalist-photographers learn in the field. It presents animal life factually as it is seen in action by our naturalist-photographers who are first of all natural scientists.

Q: Are you a music lover? I think I once heard you say that you have a tin ear. Yet you have been able to use music to such great effect.

A: Music has always had a prominent part in all our products, from the early cartoon days. So much so, in fact, that I cannot think of the pictorial story without thinking about the complementary music which will fulfill it. Often the musical theme comes first, suggesting a way of treatment. This was the case with the Tchaikovsky music for *Sleeping Beauty*, which finally formulated our presentation of the classic. I have had no formal musical training. But by long experience and by strong personal leaning, the selection of musical themes, original or adapted, we were guided to wide audience acceptance. Credit for the memorable songs and scores must of course go to the brilliant composers and musicians who have been associated with us through the years.

Q: Every animation cartoonist has learned much from you. Have you ever learned from others, such as U.P.A.?

A: Throughout the years when the art of animation was developing and going through various fashions and phases, all of us—every cartoon company—learned from one another. But once we had decided upon a format which we believed had the greatest popular appeal, we proceeded to develop it along that line toward its technical perfection and adaptation to the big screen dimensions and stereophonic sound fidelities of today's theatrical presentation. We are not influenced by the techniques or fashions of any other [motion picture] company.

Q: Do you envisage more cartoon material especially made for television?
A: There will be continued cartoon highlights in our television programs throughout the coming year. Specifically we cannot at this time indicate what they are since the schedules have not yet been determined.

Q: What is your proudest achievement?
A: The perfection of the animation art in *Sleeping Beauty*, both for its craftsmanship and story-telling power, has given all of us, as a team, the greatest satisfaction.

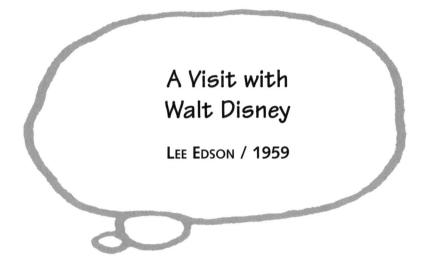

A Visit with
Walt Disney

LEE EDSON / 1959

From *Think*, May 1959, pp. 25–27.

"We have a business here we built from scratch and, boy, we had to scratch plenty," the tall sun-tanned man with the neat mustache was saying as he leaned back in his soft chair and sipped V-8 juice. We were sitting in Walt Disney's handsome office, talking across a low, square, black-topped desk, an unconventional design which the staff good-humoredly calls Disney Moderne. All around me, amid an atmosphere of subdued splendor, were mementos of Disney's versatility—a set of frontier pistols, a case of children's and nature books, a cartoon portrait of Mickey mouse and, dominating the decor, a huge aerial photo of Disneyland clamped to a wall and framed by colored posters of such fantasy and adventure pictures as *King Arthur, Down the Colorado* (both still in the dream stage) and the successful *20,000 Leagues Under the Sea*. None of these items, however, could take your eye from the master wizard himself.

At fifty-seven, Disney's brown hair is flecked with gray and his face shows a few lines of age, but he is as dynamic, imaginative, and timelessly romantic as ever. He laughs easily and heartily, and his voice is often filled with tones of eternal small-boy wonder at the miracles of life around him.

"I came here in 1923 from Kansas City and couldn't get a job," he continued. "So I went into business for myself. My brother, Roy, went in with me. We had about $750. We took a lot of bumps along the way, but we always kept striving for the same goal: How could we best use this medium of the film? How could we use this artistic talent we had developed? We were never interested in how much money we could make, only in how good a job we could do on film."

The man who has been called the most significant figure in graphic art since Leonardo da Vinci paused. "I guess we found the way all right," he said finally, with a smile. "I can make a flop now and nobody pays attention. We always have two or three other things going to save us."

Last year, Walt Disney Productions, which sprawls over fifty-one acres in Burbank, California, proved Disney's point by drawing a gross of nearly $50 million from three TV series and from a veritable tidal wave of recordings, comic books, toys, clothes, and other "character" merchandise. Also included in the figure is revenue from Disneyland, the park. Disney also runs a 16 mm. film-rental service, and he makes TV commercials for his sponsors. During the year, on top of all this, he released five full-length features.

"We're still doing a bit of everything," he told me when I asked what was coming up. "We're building a top-notch show at Disneyland called Pageant of the Presidents. It's the story of America through the Presidents, and it's got the darndest electronic system you ever saw. All you do is push a button and it takes off. It'll have full-size animated figures. No actors."

Disney jumped up from his desk and strode to the aerial view of Disneyland. "Look," he said, pointing to a spot on the photograph, his brown eyes lighting up, "you'll walk down Liberty Street and into Liberty Square. All the figures of the thirty-four Presidents will be in wax in front of you. I'll have Lincoln standing up and delivering an address. I'll have other speakers and I'll even have hecklers in the audience booing them. It'll open a year from June."

Disney returned to his desk and went on to talk volubly and enthusiastically about other Disneyland projects, including a new submarine ride—"each sub will hold forty passengers"—and a fourteen-story replica of the Matterhorn, with a real waterfall and slopes for bobsledders. "We're going to have a monorail, too," Disney added happily. "Like the one in Cologne, Germany. I just signed with Axel Wenner-Gren, the Swedish industrialist who holds the patents. You know, I think monorail is going to be the rapid transit of the future, and we'll be giving a prevue of it."

"Disneyland was a natural," Disney said reflectively. "It was so close to what we were doing in film. I thought of it a long time, but very few people believed in it at first. Now look at it. Five years ago Disneyland was just a flat plain of orange groves. It cost us $4,500 an acre. The bank recently appraised it. Know for how much? $20,000 an acre. Imagine, $20,000 an acre."

Disney paused—a bit awed, I thought, by his own swift success—and I took the opportunity to ask him about the future prospects in his major medium, the film. Was he doing more of those wonderful nature documentaries like *The Living Desert*? "We're doing True Life Adventures all the time," Disney said. "We have cameramen all over the world. Sometimes they disappoint us, though. We had one team in Australia, but they didn't come up with anything. Australia isn't a good spot for animals. No predators there. What can you do with a koala bear? He looks at you and eats a eucalyptus leaf.

"This year we've put five new films in production, including Robert Louis Stevenson's *Kidnapped* and *Toby Tyler*, the children's circus classic." Disney paused.

"You're also doing Westerns," I broke in, recalling such things as *Texas John Slaughter*. "Some people are annoyed at you for that. They think the man who produced a classic like *Fantasia* shouldn't succumb to the Western craze."

Disney shrugged. "The sponsors insist I do them. Don't get me wrong, I like a good Western, but I agree there are too many of them. Say, how about lunch?" he suddenly grinned, standing up.

"Delighted," I said, "but one question before we go. How do you manage to juggle so many things at one time and still be so good?"

Disney laughed. "I'm always close to projects when we're chewing over the basic idea," he said. "Once the pattern is set the answer to your question is simple. I let the staff take over and I go on to other things."

We walked out of the office, past a trophy case which displayed a shimmering forest of medals and plaques, including twenty-six gold Academy Awards—tangible evidence of Disney's enormous success in mingling those cultural antagonists, commerce and art. Outside at the end of Dopey Drive—the main street of the lot—we entered the Studio Restaurant, where Disney ordered only a plate of lean beef and a side dish of figs. "I'm getting my weight down," he explained with a grin. "The only exercise I get these days is walking around the lot."

As lunch proceeded I asked Disney about himself and learned that he had never finished high school, though he now holds honorary master's degrees from three universities: Harvard, Yale and Southern California. He had done illustrations for the high school paper in his native city of Chicago and had studied cartooning nights, at the Chicago Academy of Fine Arts. After World War I, he worked for an ad agency in Kansas City, made animated cartoon films for a slide company, and finally emigrated to Hollywood in 1923 with $40 in his pocket. Mickey Mouse, the only nonhuman to be immortalized in Madame Tussaud's Wax Museum, was launched in 1928 in a sound movie called *Steamboat Willie.*

The Mouse—as he's known on the lot—still remains Disney's best-known property. Disney also told me about some of his other films, and I discovered the little-known fact that he had made scores of films for industry and medical organizations on such subjects as electricity, baby feeding and the art of riveting. "We're doing some twenty-six new films for TV," he told me. "We did a short called *Mathmagic Land,* with Donald Duck, which took two years. It's tough to explain mathematics in cartoons, but I think my staff did a good job. We also just finished *Eyes in Outer Space,* a theatrical film on the weather satellite, like the film we did on the moon rocket in our science factual series."

"Do you find that TV is affecting your motion pictures in the theater?" I asked.

"Not at all," was Disney's reply. "We went into TV with one thing in mind. Not to go out of the motion picture business, but to keep the audience aware of motion pictures. We lost $2,000,000 last year in TV. But we sold our motion picture product."

By now lunch was over and we were walking back to Disney's office. I asked Disney whether in view of the low state of U.S. comedy he thought Americans were afraid to laugh, as some critics have contended. "No," Disney roared. "We just made a funny picture called *The Shaggy Dog,* which has become one of our most successful releases. Americans like to laugh. They have a sense of humor. Apropos of this, did you ever hear about the neurotic cannibal who went to see a psychiatrist? Seems he was all fed up with people."

I laughed. Disney laughed and waved good-bye. I continued down Dopey Drive, thinking that life was pretty full of joy and zest after all. Disney has that effect on you.

Interview with Stan Hellenk

STAN HELLENK / 1960

Conducted for the Canadian
Broadcasting Corporation, July 22, 1960.
Used by permission.

STAN: First, Mr. Disney, I want to thank you for giving me this time in an obviously busy schedule. Your production schedule that is coming up is quite impressive.

WALT: We have a few other things too, you know, such as Disneyland, the park. And we have a lot of planning and what we call the different stages. Imagineering is the first stage, engineering the second, and then constructing and installing the exhibits. Now that's going on at the same time, so there's never a dull moment, you might say.

STAN: Do you consider that your particular company is paradoxical in that there's so much going on here and yet we read stories where production is slackening and things are not as busy as they should be around the studios? And yet we get the impression here that you've been busier than ever before.

WALT: Well, I think it's because I'm diversified. We do television, we do the theatrical things, and again my park, the Disneyland park. I use the same talents to develop the different attractions at the park that I do to make my cartoons and make my other films here. So it was a wise move some fifteen years ago when I decided that I should diversify.

STAN: Has the evolution been a difficult thing? You foresaw that things were going to take a different track. For example the development of television. You figured, "Well, this is inevitable and I must get into it."

WALT: Yes, television will, in time, I think, become more or less an extension of the theater screen. I think there will always be things that are, say, perfect on television but could never compete on a motion picture screen. In other words, the quality of the picture—the definition and things—I don't think will ever equal that of a good high-class movie theater. But it's another way of reaching the people, another way of entertaining the people. I welcomed it. You can't fight these things. I learned that a long time ago. It's progress. You can sit back and try to fight it but it's stupid. I think, "Go with it."

STAN: Was there ever a transitory period where you had to make up your mind where the emphasis was going to be—in television production or in motion picture production—feature production? Was there ever a period where television, in a certain sense, supplanted it as your major . . .

WALT: No. I don't think television, in the foreseeable future, will supplant the motion picture theater.

STAN: I meant at a period when everybody got into a panic about television and the motion picture business and people said, "Where are we going to go? What is this thing? We gotta do something about it."

WALT: I've been in the motion picture business forty years, and in those forty years I have seen a lot of panics. I mean that thing happened when sound came in the late twenties. When sound came in with the motion picture, there was that panic then, those that said sound will never supplant the good old silent film and the public needs to let its imagination go—and all of that. But I welcomed sound. I saw another dimension with sound with my cartoons. And then the next evolution was color, and as soon as I could get three color I went to color, because again there was another dimension. Now, when television came along,

I thought it was one of the marvels of the age that entertainment could be set right into the home. And of course, I do television in a way to help me with my theatrical productions. I try to give good television programs for people who want to look in and see my programs. And while they're looking at them, I let them know about the motion pictures that I make, and I find that they appreciate it. If I have a motion picture that is a good family picture, then people want to know about it because they want to go and see it. Now, if it's one that doesn't appeal to them, no matter how many times I tell them on television, it doesn't help me. But if it's one that does have that appeal and through my television show, I let them know that I have made it, they go and see the film. So, in effect, the theatrical films that I make help subsidize my television venture because I don't make money in television. I lose money in television.

STAN: We, perhaps, can crystalize what's going to happen in the fall if you could sort of outline what the public is going to be seeing on television and at the same time what they're going to be hearing about in a feature way.
WALT: Well, it's quite a big program. I don't have my television program here. But . . .

STAN: You're going to be going on with the *Texas John Slaughter* series?
WALT: Yes, I have. This year I will have four of the *Slaughters*.

STAN: And then there's a *Daniel Boone*?
WALT: And I'm starting *Daniel Boone* with this young actor Dewey Martin, who's a real talent. I think he'll hit and I have two of the *Swamp Foxes*, but I understand that they don't like . . . they don't want me to run the *Swamp Foxes* again. [he laughs]. . . .

STAN: You have permanent offices in [the continent and the Far East]?
WALT: Oh, yeah. Offices and art staffs. We have quite an art staff in London, quite an art staff in Paris—takes care of the continent—and then we have representatives around different places. I don't know. I haven't sort of sat down and looked at that picture for a long time.

STAN: This keeps you airborne most of the year, I would think.
WALT: No. No, I'm just production. You see, that's my concern, and my my brother is president of the company. I'm not an officer of the company at all. I don't hold any office in the company. My brother is the president and chairman of the board, and he worries about the finances

and the distribution and the corporate matters. My sole concern is production—production and the show, as we call it, at Disneyland. I don't even attend the board of directors' meetings, if I can help it. It's two separate worlds, the one of production and creation, and then the business world. And my brother and I . . . Fortunately I have a brother who's been with me all these years and . . .

STAN: He has been with you constantly?
WALT: Well, yes, since I started in Hollywood. So he handles all of that. He's the financier; he's in charge of sales.

STAN: He's the fellow who tells you you're spending too much money.
WALT: Oh, constantly. Yeah, constantly. That's been the feud over the years, you know. But as a rule, though, it works out that when I spent too much money it comes back. So he don't know just where he stands, you know.

STAN: I guess the proof of the pudding is in the grosses.
WALT: Yes, yes. I remember way back when he was going crazy because I was spending twenty to thirty thousand dollars for a short subject. That was just about the time I made one that he thought was way over budget, and it was called *Three Little Pigs*.

STAN: He still remembers that?
WALT: No, he likes to forget it. That's always the constant battle. Production versus the banking side. Anybody with a banking mind . . . it must be a tangible in front of him, you know. But in our business we're dealing with intangibles which we hope to turn into tangible—two separate worlds, you might say.

STAN: Are you going to continue to concentrate on the family type entertainment in your production?
WALT: Always, I hope. I think that's the big audience, that's the audience I like to cater to. I mean that it's a natural thing for me to want to do those sort of things. I would hate to think I'd ever have to do anything I didn't have a feeling for. I don't know, I'm kind of simple and corny at heart, and I think the majority of the people are on my side.

STAN: Well, I certainly think so, Mr. Disney. And I want to thank you very much for taking this time from an obviously busy schedule. Thank you very much.
WALT: You bet.

The Wide World of Walt Disney

NEWSWEEK / 1962

In the world of children, he is the rich uncle—the casual, ordinary-looking man with the graying mustache and the baggy eyes who shows up from time to time, does funny tricks and gives wonderful presents, and then goes away until the next time. He makes everybody laugh, and everybody wonders about him—because like any proper rich uncle, he presents a fascinating mystery. Among other things, he is probably the best-known artist in the world, but he hasn't drawn a picture since 1928. He is a hugely successful businessman, but he can't be bothered with financial details and isn't even an officer in his own company. He is a Hollywood rajah who looks, talks, and lives like the owner of a Midwest hardware store.

Walter Elias Disney, sixty-one years old, has been hailed as the father of a new art form; he has also been damned as a maudlin sentimentalist who, in the words of one critic, "vulgarizes everything he touches." Lounging behind a coffee table in his Oscar-bedecked office last week, Disney made it clear that he intends to keep right on being Walt Disney. His face creased in the habitually exaggerated grin of the movie animator who has spent years studying facial expressions in his mirror, Disney sketched his idea of his job: "Our part in things is to build along the lines we are known for, with happy family stories and comedies. I've never thought of this as art. It's part of show business."

Churning On: Happily agreeing, most of the world asks only of Disney that he keep on turning out his own unique goodies—and the fantastic flow never ends. Generations of American children have laughed at Mickey Mouse and wept over Snow White. Children in Rome and Dar es Salaam read Disney comic books, and solemn Japanese children ride Dumbo elephants in a plagiarized copy of Disney's phantasmagoric amusement park. He has produced 550 motion pictures, lent his name to 2,500 books, turned out more than 600 television shows, raked in royalties on countless millions of dolls, sweatshirts, and wrist watches. But the Disney imagination, tireless as his own frenetic Donald Duck, churns on. Among the projects in various stages of planning at Disney's campuslike studio in Burbank, California:

Electronic robots. Carrying his concept of cartoon realism to what may be its ultimate point, Disney is developing life-size electronic dolls. The prototype is a figure of Abraham Lincoln, designed to recite the Gettysburg Address at Disneyland in a display to be called "One Nation Under God." This, Disney says vaguely, would include "figures of all the Presidents, who would talk to the American people and that sort of thing." The Lincoln figure operates with an intricate system of pistons geared to an electronic tape which plays the voice. The doll gestures as it talks, lips move, minute cheek muscles tighten, eyelids flutter, and individual fingers move; each of the tiny facial muscles costs $600.

Disneyland additions. Lesser robots will be featured in the "Enchanted Tiki" room, a Polynesian restaurant where diners will be entertained by audio-electronic birds and singing, dancing flowers, "I'm not in any hurry to open the room," Disney says. "Maybe we'll do it by Easter, maybe wait until June. Our ideas keep changing." Disney may also use the robots in a haunted house, replete with ogres, elves, and transparent ghosts. He has similar plans for "all of the Disney characters, so everyone can see them . . . I have in mind a theater, and the figures will not only put on the show but be sitting in the boxes with the visitors, heckling. I don't know just when I'll do that." Meanwhile, work continues on the herds of mechanical elephants, rhinoceroses, and crocodiles who already populate the park.

World's Fair exhibits. Under tight security wraps, a Disney subsidiary is working on the Ford Motor Co. and General Electric exhibits for the 1964 World's Fair in New York. "Disney seemed to be the showman to give us the package we want," says J. G. Mullaly, Ford's World's Fair program manager. "He's terrific. He's got his hands in more bowls than anyone I've ever seen, but he accomplishes what he sets out to do." One of the fair projects will probably include a 360-degree movie, adapted from the model which has been operating at Disneyland for years.

New parks. Disney has considered building an Eastern Disneyland and a theme park for Florida, without making firm plans. But he feels that the nation's "kiddielands" are ripe for a kind of Disneyland revolution—and he has definite plans to sell franchises for small child-amusement centers.

Movies. Basically, Disney says, "Our business is still making motion pictures"—about six of them each year, with one full-length animated cartoon every three years and the rest in live action. The next films due for release are *Miracle of the White Stallions*, a tale of Austria's famous Lippizzaner horses, and *Summer Magic*, a live-action family comedy. The next feature cartoon, planned for release a year hence, will be *The Sword in the Stone*, an adaptation of *The Once and Future King*, T. H. White's tender and comic novel about the education of King Arthur. In addition, seven of the classic Disney cartoons (including *Snow White*, *Cinderella*, *Pinocchio*) are on a rotating list, with one being rereleased each year.

Television. As one of his admirers puts it, Disney "makes television work for the pictures by using it to develop players and a public at the same time." This year he has a weekly, hourlong show on NBC's *Wonderful World of Color* (upcoming: *Adventures in Fantasy* and *Three Tall Tales*, featuring a cartoon version of "Casey at the Bat"), and five weekly reruns of the afternoon Mickey Mouse Club.

From his earliest days in the entertainment business, Disney has never been noted for cutting corners on production costs. His future projects will be as expensive as they are imaginative (and, some critics will inevitably charge, tasteless); the Lincoln robot, for example, has already cost more than $250,000, and Disney has no plans to exhibit it for four years. Fortunately, money is available in large, vulgar bundles—and, as Disney blandly paraphrases Thornton Wilder: "Dollars are like fertilizer— they make things grow."

The dollars come from the forty-year-old business empire known as Walt Disney Productions. In addition to the theatrical films, TV shows, and Disneyland, Disney licenses a monthly circulation of fifty million in magazines distributed in fifty countries and fifteen languages, makes television commercials and business and educational films, runs art shops, distributes songs and comic strips, and licenses hundreds of manufacturers to use the names of Disney characters in promoting their merchandise. (The usual license take: 5 percent of the wholesale price, with a guaranteed minimum of $5,000.)

The Tie-in: All these activities are firmly linked in the Disney concept of "total merchandising." As Roy Disney, Walt's sixty-nine-year-old brother and self-effacing president of the company, puts it: "Everything we do helps something else." A television show plugs a Disney movie; the movie characters can move into Disneyland or be used as the basis for more television, comics, songs, and toys. In a circle of mathematical perfection, the secondary promotions build up new interest in the movie, which can be released again. *Pinocchio*, for instance, brought the studio only $1.5 million of its $2 million production cost when first released in 1940—but two later distributions brought in $2.7 million, and a third, now in process, will return about $4 million in purest gravy.

Last year, the gravy added up to a $4.4 million profit on gross income of $70.2 million. The trend is up; last week, accountants were working on an annual report for fiscal 1962 showing the biggest gross and biggest profit in Disney's history. "It was no one thing this year," Roy Disney observes. "It was just that things were good in every capacity."

In business matters, Roy Disney is the studio's presiding genius—the man who arranges financing, works out distribution gimmicks, and prunes endlessly at costs. Without him, the studio might have foundered in any of a half-dozen fiscal crises of the past forty years. As one former Disney employee recalls: "At times it was so difficult that Roy wanted to retire, but Walt wouldn't let him. It's a lucky thing; Roy has bailed him out many times." This financial role goes so far that Walt has no corporate title at Disney Productions except his seat as one of its seven directors.

The Team: Nonetheless, Walt Disney is the total boss. Los Angeles architect William L. Pereira, a friend of both brothers, says of the relationship: "Roy has a mission which he, better than anyone else, recognizes—and that's not to check Walt, but to see to it that he has the freedom." Thus, Roy has often backed Walt in grandiose projects that looked to most of Hollywood—and to most financiers, for that matter—like reckless gambles. To build Disneyland, for instance, the brothers borrowed to the corporate hilt, and then Walt sold his vacation home at a loss and borrowed against his life-insurance policies. "My wife kept complaining that if anything happened to me I would have spent all her money," Walt recalls.

In the Disney studio, says one former animator, "it is strictly a one-man show. Walt can be kind and a dictator at the same time; in the final analysis, all ways are his ways."

Indisputably, Walt's ways work—as testified by the profit statements, twenty-nine Academy Awards, four Emmys, and seven hundred miscellaneous citations from around the world. But even his closest associates find it almost impossible to define Walt's ways, to cut through the shell of paradoxes and uncover the living man that is the true Walt Disney.

Inevitably, forty years of Hollywood have encrusted him with legends. There are the saccharine stories of studio flacks—the picture, for example, of the starry-eyed youngster who went west from Kansas City in 1923, hugging his drawing board and nursing a revolutionary dream of animated cartoons. Actually, Disney says: "I had put my drawing board away. What I wanted to do was get a job in a studio—any studio, doing anything." He came close once, landing a job as an assistant director, but the studio burned down the next day. Disney describes his next step: "When you can't get a job, you start your own business." With brother Roy and $500 borrowed from a relative, Walt did just that.

There are also the funny, malicious anecdotes which are part of the price of any Hollywood success—the story, for example, of Disney watching the rushes of *Fantasia*, reveling in the gambols of his figures and the swell of the Pastoral Symphony, and remarking earnestly: "Gee, this will *make* Beethoven." There's no way to be sure, but the odds are it never happened. As one of his animators of the era put it: "Walt was never that kind of guy. Sure, he didn't know much about music. But if there's any one thing he can do, it's recognize class when he sees it."

This instinctive recognition—of "class," and of what elements are proper to a Disney picture—is probably the most important single element in Disney's long success. (He isn't infallible, though. *Fantasia* flopped at the box office, and the Disney approach was carried so far in *Alice in Wonderland* that the story was lost in gimmicks.)

Part Children: What is a Disney picture? "Hell, I'm Disney, and I don't know," Walt said last week. "I've produced every type of picture except sick ones. The truth of the matter is, I try to make movies to please my own family. We don't aim at children specifically. When does any person stop being part child?" As for the Disney "touch," he added: "It's my group; it's group thinking. We've grown up together."

To his artists and writers, though, the street is one-way. "If Walt doesn't like it, it isn't good," one long-time employee says wryly. And Disney is formidable in the pursuit of his own interior vision. A driving perfectionist, he spent $500,000 in remaking the entire battle with the giant squid in *20,000 Leagues Under the Sea* and forced his sculptors to make 175 boy-size models of Pinocchio before he was satisfied.

Disney is equally tenacious in developing ideas. He first thought of Disneyland, for example, some thirty years ago; the project would lie dormant for a year or two, flower into new plans and sketches, and drop nearly out of sight. "It's trial and error," Disney says. "Try out ideas. Throw out the old and search for something better. Take it back and 'hypo' the act."

"I saw very early in this business one thing—that organization was where you had to put the emphasis," Disney says. "You have to break things down, specialize." Partly for this reason, Disney himself hasn't drawn anything at all since 1928. "I don't doodle; I've never drawn anything for my grandchildren," he says. "I've got too many good artists around here. If they got hold of some drawing I'd done, I'd be in trouble."

As chief organizer, Disney puts in a fourteen-hour day in his four-room office, in story conferences and projection rooms, and in long, rambling tours of the studio. Dressed usually in open-neck sports shirts, sweater, and slacks, he pauses for brief dialogues with directors, animators, secretaries, and machinists. "It could be a little startling," one ex-staffer recalls. "He might want to talk about what you were doing, but he might just as easily say, 'Gee, did you see those northern lights last night?' "

At the end of the day, Disney frequently takes movie scripts and films to his comfortable, antique-filled home in Holmby Hills and sits alone with his wife, Lillian, reading or editing (their two daughters are married, and the Disneys have five grandchildren). He makes no effort to keep up with the movie colony, dines at the least fashionable places, and washes dishes with other do-gooders after parties at Los Angeles's Children's Hospital.

The Paradox: In fact, Walt Disney conveys an implacably commonplace impression. He tends to moodiness (in the morning, the story goes, studio staffers gather at the window to watch Walt walk in; if he smiles at the guard, things will probably be OK). But his moods are trifling in the supercharged atmosphere of Hollywood. He's been known for years as a low-pay man and a ruthless molder of talent; one of his ex-animators, cartoonist Virgil Partch, has called him "the de Gaulle of the cartoon world." But most of the artists who have worked for him went there mainly for the experience—and, as Partch says: "It's one of the world's best art schools." In fact, Disney is a pretty good boss. (Whether they like it or not, his employees are expected to call him Walt—including the guard at the gate.) Most of his top aides have been with him since the late 1930s, and those who left show few hard feelings. Perhaps his only conspicuous trait is his capacity for total preoccupation. One associate recalls him pondering a problem and absently dipping a doughnut in his Scotch.

But Disney isn't a commonplace man—and in groping for the elusive key to his character, the men who know him come up with wildly contradictory appraisals. "He's simple, uncomplicated, a real person," says Technicolor vice president George Murphy. "Walt *is* about as childlike as an electronic computer," snorts a former employee. "He has a universal language," says architect Pereira. "He's never quite listening to what you say," observes actor Fred MacMurray.

In Hiding: In the end, Disney himself provides the best clue. When he returned to his boyhood home in Marceline, Missouri, to dedicate a school named after him, he said: "I'm not modest. I'm scared. I'm not funny. I hide behind the mouse, the duck, and a lot of other things." And when he's asked what he wants, he says: "All I try to do and hope for is to do as well in the future as I've done in the past." Why should Disney hide? A penetrating answer from Walt Kelly, creator of *Pogo* and another Disney alumnus: "He has great sensitivity to people in the mass. He knows, instinctively, how to reach Mr. and Mrs. America; he's a great entertainer. But he can't get close to people as individuals. Sure, he only wants to make good movies—that's all he can do."

One day last week, the ordinary-looking man with the graying mustache stood alone near a turnstile at Disneyland, watching the customers explore his latest goody—a seventy-foot tree house, built on three levels and festooned with steps and galleries. The customers liked it—the furnishings, the steps, the view from the top—and so, still alone, the world's rich uncle smiled and walked away.

Interview with
Fletcher Markle

FLETCHER MARKLE / 1963

Aired on September 25, 1963, on
Telescope, a television show written,
produced, and hosted by Fletcher Markle
for the Canadian Broadcasting
Corporation, used by permission.

FLETCHER: Walt, you're a man who's famous for many things. . . . not the least of which is building a better mouse. And the world has been beating a path to your door for thirty-five years. I'm dating the beginning of that path, of course, from 1928 and the release of *Steamboat Willie*, the picture that introduced sound to the cartoon and Mickey Mouse to the world. Was this actually the first cartoon in which Mickey appeared?
WALT: Well, yes, in which Mickey appeared, yes, but I was making cartoons long before that. In fact, I think I've been in this business as long as anybody living today. I started, actually, to make my first animated cartoons in 1920. Of course, they were very crude things then and I

89

used . . . oh sort of little puppet things. We didn't draw them like we do today. I used to make little cut-away things and joints were pinned and we'd put them under the camera and we'd maneuver them and we'd make him do things.

FLETCHER: This was before you came to Hollywood?
WALT: Oh yes. This started back in Kansas City, Missouri, where I was making little advertisements for theaters. It's equivalent to what you see in TV commercials today. You know, "Put your winter coal in early." "Get your Fedora blocked for the winter" and all those kind of things. [Fletcher laughs and Walt continues.]
WALT: "Get your . . ." oh, this was back in the days when they had the old canvas tops on cars. "Get your top renewed."

FLETCHER: That's still necessary, of course.
WALT [laughing]: Yeah, and there was one little thing I did . . . you had to think up little gags, little catch things, you know. So I had this spanking, shining car drive in and I had a character on the street. He hailed the driver and he says, "Hi, old top, new car?" and the guy in the car says, "No old car, new top."
[They both laugh; Walt continues.]
WALT: Then we go into the pitch of where to get them renewed.

FLETCHER: Well, I was dating Steamboat Willie simply because it was Mickey's first appearance and also the first introduction of sound to the cartoon. Now in the case of Steamboat Willie I suppose sometimes picture came first and sometimes sound came first, or was it always picture?
WALT: No, in the days of Steamboat Willie it was picture first. And then we used to put the sound on afterwards, and in those days you couldn't do what we call "dubbing" today where you could mix a lot [of] tracks. It wasn't yet a science that you could get away with so we used to have to do everything at one time. And we used to have to run the cartoon. We'd have the fellows with the sound effects. We had the people with the voices. We had the orchestra going and everybody had to synchronize to keep that thing right on the button. We had a way of doing it though. We had a little kind of a beat that worked up and down and it was so many of those beats you know (and they were all musicians working for me). So they could follow those beats and when it came to a certain number of beats they would go "up" [here Walt gestures with his hands], or they would go "bang" or they would "this" [gestures

again] or they would pop one of those popguns, you know, and they would always fit.

FLETCHER: My, it was kind of opening night for everybody, wasn't it?
WALT: Oh yes, it was a madhouse.

FLETCHER: And after *Steamboat Willie*, of course, came the Silly Symphonies. So many of them, so happily remembered, and not quite ten years after *Steamboat Willie*, we saw *Snow White and the Seven Dwarfs*. The first feature-length cartoon.
WALT: Yes, just about ten years.

FLETCHER: How long was it in production, Walt?
WALT: I actually started to plan the picture about 1935. And I fooled around with it trying to get a hold of a story and things for a couple of years and finally it began to jell. Then I went to work on it and I finished it the fall of 1938. I didn't know what I had or what would happen or anything. We had the family fortune . . . we had everything wrapped up in *Snow White*. In fact the banker, I think, was losing more sleep than I was. And fortunately, though, when we put it in and premiered it and everything else, why everything was just fine and the banker was happy.

FLETCHER: And the following spring, along came that Academy Award.
WALT: Oh, yeah.

FLETCHER: In eight parts.
WALT: It wasn't but about two years later that I was almost broke.

FLETCHER: Two years later was following *Pinocchio* and coming into the *Fantasia*.
WALT: Yeah, that about did it, you know.
[Fletcher and Walt both laugh.]

FLETCHER: But that was another one . . .
WALT: Artistic success, financial failure.

FLETCHER: Certainly an artistic success. It was magnificent.
WALT: Well, there's some people that would question that too.

FLETCHER: And I recall a new and musical Mickey standing in for Leopold Stokowski.
WALT: Well, that's what started it. I was doing this *Sorcerer's Apprentice* with Mickey Mouse, and I happened to have dinner one night with

Stokowski. And Stokowski said, "Oh, I'd love to conduct that for you." Well, that led to not only doing this one little short subject but it got us involved to where I did all of *Fantasia* and before I knew it I ended up spending four hundred and some odd thousand dollars getting music with Stokowski.

[They laugh and Walt continues.]

WALT: But we were in then, and it was the point of no return. We went ahead and made it.

FLETCHER: Well, it was certainly worth it. Every foot of the way.

WALT: He's a great guy though. I don't want to belittle Stokowski, but he is a great musician, a great artist.

FLETCHER: Well perfectionism always costs money, I guess, and that's certainly something you've always been after.

WALT: I was always known as the perfectionist until I met Stokowski.

FLETCHER: Then you had a new member of the club. I see.

[Walt and Fletcher both laugh, and Fletcher continues with his interview.]

FLETCHER: About a year after the release of *Fantasia*, Robert Benchley, I remember, joined you in explaining to audiences all over the world how you go about making a cartoon. What are the principal technical advances since that time?

WALT: Better drawing. The first thing I did when I got a little money to experiment, I put all my artists back in school. The art schools that existed then didn't quite have enough for what we needed so we set up our own art school.

FLETCHER: You were inventing a new art anyway.

WALT: Well, yes, but we were just going a little bit beyond what they were getting in the art school where they worked with the static figure. Now we were dealing in motion, movement and flow of movement, the flow of things. Action, reaction, and all of that. So we had to set up our own school, and out of that school have come the artists that now make up my staff here. And, more than that, the artists that make up almost all of the cartoon outfits in Hollywood were directly or indirectly out of my school.

FLETCHER: Of course, everything is people, and it was the individual and collective talents of these artists. I was only asking if there had been a

technical advance in that your own work in the cartoon field seems to have acquired so much more depth and much more . . .
WALT: Yes, there are many technical advances, but basically the thing that gives you depth is the ability to draw the way it should be drawn for this medium. You get a lot of depth out of the way you shape a line, the way you draw a figure. That contributes an awful lot to the depth and to the overall effect that you see today with the cartoon.

FLETCHER: Now in the early 1940s we saw *Saludos Amigos* and a little later *The Three Caballeros*, the latter being the first combination of live action and cartoon. Tell us a little about how these two pictures came into being.
WALT: Which one? *Saludos Amigos* and . . .

FLETCHER: That, I presume, kind of led you to *The Three Caballeros*.
WALT: Well, I was asked by the government to go to South America as kind of a cultural thing, you know, before the Nazi days. And I went down to the staff to see if I couldn't make some film about the ABC countries down there. There's Argentina, Brazil, and Chile. They first wanted me to go on a hand-shaking good will tour, and I said I didn't go for that. I'm not a hand-shaker. So then they came back and said, "Well, you go down and make some films about these countries," and I said, "Well, that's my business, I can do that."

FLETCHER: Take a pencil in your hand.
WALT: That's right. So I took a staff and we set up headquarters in Rio; we also set up a studio in the Argentine. We went over to Chile and some of my artists . . . we divided a party—some of them went up through Peru. And when we came back I made these four short subjects. We brought back the "Tiko, Tiko" tune that was being played then. We brought that back and put it in. We brought back "Brazil" and both of them became standard tunes here, and out of it we developed this little Brazilian parrot "José Carioca," who played with Donald Duck, and these four films were more or less put together and went out in the theaters. Of course, there was one of those things, they thought Disney needed a subsidy, but you know fortunately that little thing went out and it did a heck of a business and the U.S. Government didn't have to put up one nickel.

FLETCHER: Wonderful!
WALT: It was actually a good will tour for the government.

FLETCHER: It was later, about two years later, that the three caballeros then became the new caballeros.
WALT: That was a follow-up . . .

FLETCHER: . . . combining live action.
WALT: Yeah, I almost needed a subsidy on that one.
[Fletcher laughs.]

FLETCHER: I gather that *Mary Poppins*, currently in production, is a further development of the combination live action and cartoon.
WALT: Yes, you might say that. We have a sequence in *Mary Poppins* where we have the live characters in with the animated drawings. But basically *Mary Poppins* is a live musical fantasy. The whole story is carried out by live actors, and of course, we have a lot of tricks of the trade here that we incorporated into *Mary Poppins*, such as they fly around and all that kind of stuff, you know, but basically it is still live action, musical fantasy. With a wonderful cast, by the way.

FLETCHER: Let's change the subject for a few minutes, Walt, from film activities to outside activities. Perhaps I should say outdoors activities. I'd like to talk to you about Disneyland. Where did you originally get the first notion for Disneyland?
WALT: Well, it came about when my daughters were very young, and Saturday was always Daddy's day with the two daughters. So we'd start out and try to go someplace, you know, different things, and I'd take them to the merry-go-round and I took them different places and as I'd sit while they rode the merry-go-round and did all these things—sit on a bench, you know, eating peanuts—I felt that there should be something built, some kind of an amusement enterprise where the parents and the children could have fun together. So that's how Disneyland started. It took many years. It was a period of maybe fifteen years developing. I started with many ideas, threw them away, started all over again. And eventually it evolved into what you see today at Disneyland. But it all started from a Daddy with two daughters wondering where he could take them where he could have a little fun with them too.

FLETCHER: Now that Disneyland is flourishing as a place of dreams coming true, who goes to Disneyland? What is the ratio of adults to children as part of the plan of father and daughters?
WALT: Oh, it's four adults to one child. That is, we're counting the teenagers as adults.

FLETCHER: Of course.

WALT: In the winter time you can go out there during the week and you won't see any children. You'll see all the oldsters out there riding all these rides and having fun and everything. Summertime, of course, the average would drop down. But the overall year round average is four adults to one child.

FLETCHER: And, of course, in my knowledge there's only been one adult whose been refused permission to the park.

WALT: No. We didn't refuse him permission. No, we were all set. You see, we work according to what the State Department wants to do when they have guests. Khrushchev was a guest of the government, so, I mean we were ready to receive Khrushchev. But it so happened that the security problem here in Los Angeles . . . because, actually, Disneyland is in another county, you see . . . and the Chief of Police, we can't blame him. He had quite a chore there to carry out. He just was a little worried about somebody maybe walking in Disneyland with a shopping bag and what they might have in it you'd never be able to know. But we were ready for him. The press was ready. Both the State Department security and the Soviet security had come and cased Disneyland, and they were all set. And I was all ready. In fact we've had a lot of dignitaries down there, and he was one that Mrs. Disney wanted to go down and meet. So, she was disappointed he didn't come.

[Fletcher and Walt both laugh heartily.]

FLETCHER: Well, it's certainly not ever an empty place, so I can understand the security men's concern.

WALT: We had different shots, places where we'd take pictures with Khrushchev, and I had one that was my favorite. We'd lined up in front of my eight submarines, you see, and I thought it'd be nice. I'd be pointing to Mr. Khrushchev and saying, "Well now, Mr. Khrushchev, here's my Disneyland submarine fleet."

[They both laugh again and Walt continues, still on camera.]

WALT: It's the eighth largest submarine fleet in the world.

FLETCHER: Is it really?

WALT: Uh huh.

FLETCHER: Well, we're going to be seeing part of the tour that the submarines make, presently, so it's interesting to hear about. What was the initial cost of the Disneyland that first saw the light of day?

WALT: Oh, it goes back so far. I had different cost estimates. One time it was three and a half million, and then I kept fooling around with it and it got up to seven and a half million, and I kept fooling around a little more and pretty soon it was twelve and a half, and I think when we opened Disneyland it was seventeen million dollars.

FLETCHER: And then it grew like topsy till . . .
WALT: Today it's going on forty-five million dollars.

FLETCHER: My goodness! Well, now today the newest and most exciting aspect of Disneyland is—I turned this over on my tongue several times—what you call Audio-Animatronics.
WALT: Yes, Audio-Animatronic figures. It's a sort of another door that's opened for us. You see our whole forty some odd years here has been in the world of making things move. Inanimate things move. From a drawing through all kinds of any little props and things. Now we're making these human figures, dimensional human figures, move, making animals move, making anything move through the use of electronics. It's a tape mechanism that is like the programming, or sequencing, when they do a missile, when they're sending some missile to the moon, say. At different stages, at different times, things must happen. That's all predetermined. So our show is put on that tape, and it's programmed from this tape and we run it off a little one-inch tape that has fourteen tracks and on each track we can get up to sixteen signals. Now those little signals go and impulse this figure and make the figure move and make the figure talk and everything. Well, look. I could show it to you a lot better than I can tell you.
[Walt begins to rise from his chair at the desk.]
Look, will you come over here and I'll give you a little preview.

FLETCHER [rising from chair]: I should say.
[Walt and Fletcher go to a table with two hand grips, parrot and a robin on it.]
WALT: Here we are, Fletcher. This is a little audio-animatronic set-up with parlor kit.

FLETCHER: What have we here?
[Walt motions to the two birds on the table.]
WALT: A parlor kit, so to speak. Now these are not working from tape. These are manually controlled. This little gizmo here, kinda like a joy stick on the old type airplanes, is what gives us a chance to program the

birds, and as we work this and get all the little movements that we want in the bird out, we record it on the tape and from then on the tape will do everything that we've done here.

[Walt and Fletcher sit down at the table and Walt points to robin.]

WALT: Sit down and we'll have a little go at this thing. Now this is not part of our Disneyland show. I mean you know the Tiki Room. This is a little robin that we had in *Mary Poppins*.

[Walt takes handle and makes the robin move.]

WALT: And this little bird sang a duet with Julie Andrews. Maybe we can get a little response from it. Hello there. Kid, what can you do for us, eh? Can you sing, whistle . . . anything?

[Robin whistles. Walt and Fletcher laugh.]

FLETCHER: That's marvelous!

WALT: Now this is one of the characters from the Tiki Room. He's actually a substitute, if one of our master of ceremonies . . . we have four macaws who act as master of ceremonies in the Tiki Bird Room at Disneyland. They actually keep the show rolling. And along with them are other birds who sing and things and flowers that sing. Then the Tiki images, you know. The carved Tiki poles and things. And these Tiki Gods, they sing and they drum and we have quite a show.

[Walt starts working the parrot's handle.]

Walt: But this is the boy that takes care of it. He has another word. He's the stand-in for one of 'em, you know.

FLETCHER: He's alert.

WALT: [Walt laughs] Throw out your chest. Show them how big. That's it. Now this is Fletcher Markle of CBC.

PARROT: I'm sorry I didn't catch the name.

FLETCHER: Markle.

PARROT: How do you spell that sir?

FLETCHER: M . . . A . . . R . . . K . . . L . . . E . . .

PARROT: M . . . A . . . R . . . K . . . Markle.

FLETCHER: That's right.

PARROT: How do you do, sir?

FLETCHER: How do you do? Uh . . . whatever your name is.

PARROT: Uh . . . Walt. What is my name?

WALT: Well, to tell you the truth we haven't given him a name yet. How would you like José?

PARROT: Uh . . . Uh . . . Muchas gracias. This gives me an accent.

[Walt laughs.]

FLETCHER: How do you do, José? Now it's official.

PARROT: How do you do? Oh, I missed my accent.

WALT: Well, that's just a little demonstration of Audio-Animatronic figures.

FLETCHER: Now let me make sure I understand what happens in controlling these birds by these extraordinary instruments. You can, at the same time, record their movements on a tape?

WALT: That's right. After we get it, we get it programmed. It's like rehearsing a show when you go through it and rehearse it and rehearse it and you finally say, "That's it." We say, "All right, let's go for a take." All the things we do here are recorded, and then when we play the tape back he will do everything he is doing here. Only it is all part of a programmed show, you see.

FLETCHER: I understand then that the next step beyond the birds has been to do the same kind of programming with human beings.

WALT: Yes, with human beings. Yes. Not going to replace the human being—believe me on that.

[Fletcher laughs.]

WALT: Just for show purposes, because now you take Disneyland down there. We operate fifteen hours a day. And these shows have to go on the hour. And my Tiki bird show goes on three times an hour, and I don't have to stop for coffee breaks and all that kind of stuff, you see. So that's the whole idea of it. It's just another dimension in the animation we have been doing all our life. It's a dimensional thing and it's a new door. It's a new toy for us and we are having a lot of fun. We hope we can really do some exciting things in the future.

FLETCHER: May I try one here?

[Fletcher plays with robin as Walt leans toward it.]

WALT: Why don't you go right ahead? How about a song there?

[Robin whistling.]

WALT: What about you, José? You got anything to say?

[Fletcher laughs.]

PARROT: Hasta la vista.

[Walt laughs.]
WALT: That's right. Hasta la vista. Let's go over and finish our tea.

FLETCHER: Good enough. Walt, let's change the subject again, if we may. I would like to ask you now about your accomplishments as an international film producer. You've made films in how many countries in the world?
WALT: Oh, I can't recall 'cause we've done a lot of our nature films, and we've had a series called *People and Places* where we went all over Japan and different places, even over into Egypt. But I have been basically making films in England. First with our British company, and then in Canada.

FLETCHER: Our *Telescope* viewers are naturally interested in your plans for Canada. They remember, *Niki, the Wild Dog of the North*, which I think was your first Canadian production.
WALT: Yes, we did that between Calgary and Banff, and we worked with the Canadian Wildlife . . . what would you call it? Canadian Wildlife . . .

FLETCHER: Society, I guess.
WALT: Is it society? No, it's the government. It's the government. Anyway they let us have an experimental station that was abandoned, that they weren't using, and we put a company there and they went right through the winter and we got some wonderful stuff on the film.

FLETCHER: And then with the second film, you went to eastern parts to make *Big Red*.
WALT: Uh hum.

FLETCHER: Coming up in the next few days Canadians are going to be seeing your third Canadian production, *The Incredible Journey*.
WALT: That's Sheila Burnford's best selling story, one of my favorites. I think the animals in that are terrific. I hate to say that to you, Fletcher, because you directed the humans. [Walt laughs.] I'm always partial to animal actors, anyway.
[Fletcher laughs.]
WALT: You know.

FLETCHER: Well, I found the animals pretty pleasant too, I must say. But it's certainly the animals' picture and one of the most remarkable animal stories of its kind that I've ever read, let alone had anything to do with

as a film. I gather, Walt, that you first found out about the story even before it was published in North America.
WALT: Yes.

FLETCHER: During its English publication.
WALT: Yes. It was first published in England; and that's where we caught on to it.

FLETCHER: You had your plans long before it became a best seller.
WALT: Yes. We got into quite a hassle. Some bidding went on to get that story and it all ended up and I found out it was my good friend George Seaton who was bidding against me. [Walt laughs.] George apologized, he said, "I'm sorry I ran the price up on you, Walt, but I didn't know you were bidding against me."

FLETCHER: These are the things you can never know about in advance. Actually, the part of the Canadian story that interests me more than any other is the fact that your father was born in Canada and lived a good part of his life there before he moved to parts of the south and began producing sons.
WALT: Yes, he was born in a little town, I think they call it Bluevale. It's right out of Goderich. The Disney family were Anglo-Irish, and they migrated over there in the 1830s, which makes me feel that the Disneys had foresight because it was 1840 when they had the potato famine in Ireland. But they were smart enough to get out before that. And my father was born there and he was raised there, went to school there—in fact he went to school in Goderich. He was about twenty years old when my grandfather went to Kansas . . . out in the same area where General Eisenhower, ex-president Eisenhower, came from, and he was an alien, of course, being a Canadian. And he had to buy his land. He couldn't homestead. And he bought a section of railroad land and that property stayed with the Disney family until just a few years ago. And my uncle had it, and and I told him, "Before you sell, let us know." And so finally he wanted to sell it and retire. And I went to my brother and said, "Let's buy, this virgin land that our ancestors acquired and he said, "What do we want with farming land?" He wouldn't go with me, so I didn't go ahead. I found out later that they struck gas and oil on it. [Walt laughs.]

FLETCHER: Well, you can't win them all!
WALT: NO!!! [He laughs.]

FLETCHER: Tell me, Walt, have you been back to your father's homestead at all in recent years?

WALT: My father and I had planned to go back 'cause as a boy my father always told me about his boyhood in Canada. And you see here fourth of July is a big deal here, but my father always referred to the Queen's birthday, and that was Victoria, and that was when they had their big doings. I always wanted to go up there with my father because he told me about all these different things that he did as a youngster. And the country. He thought it was the most beautiful country in the world. And yet he came down here to live. He died before we had a chance to do that.

FLETCHER: After your father's death, did you finally get a chance to get back up to the old homestead?

WALT: Yes, I finally made it. I took Mrs. Disney along and—she's not too interested in ancestors and things, you know—we got up there, and she really fell in love with the town of Goderich. It was a beautiful town, and she was quite happy about it. But I wanted to find the homestead where my grandfather went out and cut the trees down and pulled the rocks apart, where my father was born. So they gave me directions, and every-body was trying to be helpful and everything. Mrs. Disney reluctantly went along. And I found this old place and I said, "This is it . . . there." It was really deserted. There were cows running through the house and chickens around and I had my camera, and I got out and photographed that thing from every angle. When I got through, I found out I had pho-tographed the wrong homestead. [Walt laughs.] Ever since, Mrs. Disney has never forgot. She tells that to everybody. About when Walt went up to Canada and he photographed the wrong homestead.

FLETCHER: Well, let's leave that in the past where it properly belongs and look ahead for a moment to the future, Walt. What's on your immediate schedule? I gather there are some projects for the World's Fair in New York.

WALT: Yes. They're more or less an extension of Disneyland in a way. We are doing four shows for the World's Fair.

FLETCHER: Four?

WALT: Yes, about fifty million dollars' worth of shows that we are doing for the World's Fair. Of course, that includes the cost of building and rent of the land and everything. We are doing one for the Ford Motor Company. We are doing one for General Electric. We are doing one for the Pepsi-Cola Company and the State of Illinois.

FLETCHER: When you say extensions of Disneyland, are any of them Audio-Animatronic?

WALT: Yes. Audio-Animatronic and dimensional type of shows like we do at Disneyland. Not film shows. There is no film involved in any of these shows. We use Audio-Animatronic figures and at the State of Illinois exhibit we are going to have great moments with Mr. Lincoln. Mr. Lincoln is going to be there. He's going to speak five times an hour. He's going to be very life-like and very, very believable. And we're finding some wonderful words of Mr. Lincoln that are still prophetic today. And I think it's going to be a great moment for the public when they can sit and hear Mr. Lincoln talk about some of the things. What is liberty? You know. The rights and the obligations that we have and all of that. I think it's needed today, too.

FLETCHER: I should say it is. Well, Walt, it's very difficult to talk about rewards because certainly you've had so many of them. Twenty-nine Oscars, and nearly seven hundred awards from all corners of the world. But, personally, what has been your greatest reward to date?

WALT: Well, my greatest reward, I think, is that I've been able to build this wonderful organization. I've been able to enjoy good health, and the way I feel today, I feel like I can still go on being a part of this thing after forty some odd years of the business, and also to have the public appreciate and accept what I've done all these years. That is a great reward.

FLETCHER: I'm sure it is. It seems unlikely, but if you had it to do over again would you do any part of it differently?

WALT: If I had it to do over again, no, I don't think I would. [Walt laughs.] I don't know. I hope I don't have to do it over again. [Walt and Fletcher both laugh.]

FLETCHER: There's certainly a completely unique reward in having that feeling about your work and what you've accomplished.

WALT: Yes.

FLETCHER: That's a reward of satisfaction and happiness, surely.

WALT: Yes.

FLETCHER: What does happiness mean to you, Walt?

WALT: Well, of course, happiness is a state of mind. You can be happy or you can be unhappy. It's just according to the way you look at things.

You know. So I think happiness is contentment but it doesn't mean you have to have wealth. But all individuals are different. Some of us wouldn't be satisfied with just carrying out a routine job and being happy. Yet I envy those people. I had a brother who I really envied because he was a mailman. But he was the one who had all the fun. He had himself a trailer, and he used to go out and go fishing. He didn't worry about pay-rolls and stories and picture grosses or anything. And he was the happy one. I always said, "He's the smart Disney."
[Walt and Fletcher both laugh.]

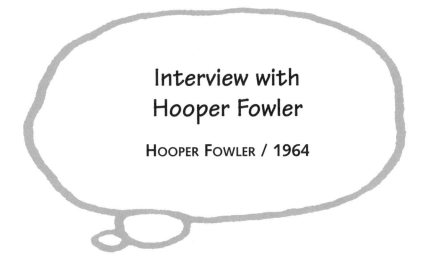

Interview with Hooper Fowler

HOOPER FOWLER / 1964

Thirty-minute interview done for
Look Magazine, January 1964.

FOWLER: Isn't it a fact, sir, that you have selected and decided upon most of your major themes rather than getting them through a research department?

WALT: No, some of the things we more or less built from scratch, as you'd say. Some of them, we'd find a little idea that acts as a spring board to develop into a full motion picture. Two of our most successful films here were *The Absent-Minded Professor* and the more or less sequel to it called *The Son of Flubber*. Both of those were, you might say, wholly created here in the studio but we had a springboard. We had a little idea that—well, one of them I read in the old *Liberty Magazine*. It was just a little short story about somebody that invented a certain substance that we turned into what we called flubber. From there, we built the whole thing. But in other cases, we have taken some of the classic things, like the Jules Verne stories and built them into very successful pictures.

And one of our most successful here was called *The Parent Trap* and that sprung off of an idea by a German author by the name of Kästner. It was about identical twins and their problem of bringing their parents together. We transplanted it over here and built it into an entirely different story, in effect, and it was very successful.

No, you need good story ideas. We buy them; some of them we invent, or they're based on old classics that we kind of bring up to date, but they're awful hard to find, the good ones. There are a lot of stories today that wouldn't do for our audience. We have a very broad audience. We call it the family audience. In fact, it's been said that we make films that children are not embarrassed to take their parents to. But that's a very important part of the movie audience that has been neglected through these recent years, where the downbeat and the oversexed type of things have been predominating.

FOWLER: May, I ask you one question relating to that, Mr. Disney? Do you receive or your reading department, or whatever, any suggestions from writers in New York and writers working abroad in the course of the year?
WALT: Well, most of the writers work through their publishers. So, we have our story editor in New York, a story department here, and we have our department in London. Through London comes everything that is printed on the continent. It comes to London; it is analyzed in London. So, we're constantly on the lookout for things that would fit into our type of presentations. The writers seem to be off on a binge. And Hollywood, as the rule, goes by the way the publishing business goes. So I think that's contributed to the trend in Hollywood. But we've still managed to come up with a few things that Hollywood classifies as untouchables, that we've been able to swing around and turn into, what I call, very good Disney property.

FOWLER: Can you give me an example of that, sir? The "untouchable?"
WALT: Well, yes, there are several things here that have been lying around for an awful long time. *Swiss Family Robinson*—they made one a good many years ago, and it was a flop, and it's just seemed to beat the boo in Hollywood. But I tried to get a hold of it—took quite awhile

because somebody had it, and I had to clear it. And finally did clear it, and I made it into a very successful film.

FOWLER: How often do you go to Disneyland now, Mr. Disney?

WALT: Oh, I might average once a month. Most of my interest in Disneyland is planning and improving it, and I do a great deal of that here at the studio. So I only go down to check on things, to see what ought to be done for the coming year. It's pretty hard to get around Disneyland when people are there. I mean, they're friendly, they're wonderful, and I love to meet them, but I can't stand still long because I'll— oh, I don't mind giving autographs; I think it's wonderful that they do want your autograph. But when I'm at Disneyland, if I stop to sign one autograph, before I can get that signed, there are some more up there, and it accumulates quite a crowd, and it always makes it awful hard to get away.

So when I go through Disneyland, I walk fast, and it isn't much fun. So I go down with my staff when Disneyland is closed, and we go through everything. Or I go down when there is a big crowd, a very big crowd, and I walk very fast and watch every part of it and find out

Sleeping Beauty Castle, opening day at Disneyland˙ Park, © Disney Enterprises, Inc.

where we need to improve our crowd control conditions to make it easier for people to get around and our shade areas and all the problems that we have in the summer when we have the half million plus people a week.

So mainly my interest in Disneyland has been building that thing, in keeping it alive and keeping it fresh and keeping it successful by doing these things. So most of my fun comes from that end of it.

FOWLER: I read in an article that you had spent $25 million in additional entertainment values since the original investment. Is that correct, sir?

WALT: Yes, that is, the Studio has, that's not my personal money. It started out, I think the initial investment was about $17 million and we really had to scratch to get that. Since then, I think we're well up to over $40 million. But it's been our policy here to reinvest. And everything that is earned here by pictures, or in any other way, always goes back into the business, goes back to improve our studio facilities, to improve the operations of any one of these things, like Disneyland. It's always going back into the business.

I know different ways of looking at things. I have my stockholders, and I feel a very keen responsibility to the stockholders, but I feel that the main responsibility I have to them is to have the stock appreciate. And you only have it appreciate by reinvesting as much as you can back in the business. And that's what we've done.

FOWLER: Their dividends this year should have been satisfactory.

WALT: Well, this year we give them stock dividends. And stock dividends to a lot of people who own stock is preferrable to cash because you don't have to pay your income tax on a stock dividend until you finally sell the stock. And the stock can appreciate. And by giving them a stock dividend, we retain the money in the business, to keep building the business. And that has been my philosophy on running the business.

FOWLER: Will there ever be another Disneyland? Or will that take the fun out of it?

WALT: I think there will only be one Disneyland as such. Now, that doesn't mean that in some areas we might not develop certain projects that would be compatible to that area, that might very well tie in certain historical themes of the area of things like that and we are considering things of that sort. Because we do know that this is a big country. We're going to have two hundred million people here pretty soon and surveys have shown that we draw from about fifty million of that two hundred million. That is, most of the people to Disneyland, the big percentage is coming west of the Mississippi and more or less the Pacific coast. The great center of the population is east of the Mississippi, and it's possible that we could go to these areas with certain things without in any way depreciating the individuality of Disneyland itself.

But there will only be one Disneyland as such. It's quite a chore to keep Disneyland going. It's like a big show you've got to keep on the road, you know. You've got to keep it fresh and new and exciting. And when people come back, you always want to have something new they hadn't had a chance to see before. And we feel a keen responsibility to the customer there. They aren't customers, we call them paying guests.

FOWLER: Now, to insure this in your own mind, you must also spend a great deal of time in personnel considerations. The people who are going to be useful for this and this so that the continued progress is guaranteed. Is that one of your major considerations?
WALT: Well, we try to set up a good, strong, fair administrating organization. I try to have good people in each spot. Then I expect those people to do the job. Now, fortunately in the Disneyland setup I've got some wonderful people there. We have some wonderful policies set for the employees and we see that all these things are part of it. And the consideration of the employee is very important. That's why we have a thing called friendliness and cleanliness. The employee must reflect that if you want the people to feel it. And if we find somebody sometime who just doesn't have the knack of making himself friendly to the crowd, why we find him another spot where he doesn't have to meet the public.

FOWLER: I wanted to ask you that. I've seen young people—and by young people, I mean young men apparently eighteen or nineteen years old with the combination of authority and warmth that some of those kids have during the summer season. There's no questions about you following their directions and yet they do not press you. How do they train?
WALT: Well, we do have to put on a staff of about—the staff in the winter time is about a thousand. Then I think we have to go well over three thousand in the summer, because we're running seven days a week and fifteen hours a day. And they're recruited from all over. We get applications from college students and from teachers and vice principals and people like that, who want to come and work for the summer. And when they do, we have what we call the University of Disneyland where

those that are accepted are put on a two week basis of going through this University where they learn all about how to handle the public and our attitude toward the public.

And they come out of there with quite an education on how to win friends and influence people. It's a well-laid out course. They're indoctrinated into the whole philosophy of our operation. They're even brought to our studio to become made familiar with the studio because the questions are asked about the studio.

FOWLER: Now let me ask you this question, sir, and we can skip it if it's a headache, or record it if it is not. How would a young man in Kansas City, or Waukegan or Rochester go about applying as a candidate for that training course? Would he have a recommendation from his school or how could he do that?
WALT: He'd have to send us some credentials or something to give us his background.

FOWLER: To whom?
WALT: To the Personnel Director at Disneyland.

FOWLER: And such a query would be considered?
WALT: Oh yes, and is always answered.

FOWLER: Now, if you want to, I'd like to talk about *Fantasia*. I think *Look Magazine* called it your only flop, and Joe Reddy corrected me and said it was qualified success. Are there things about *Fantasia*, anecdotes or correspondence that you've learned and comments you've heard that the general public is not aware of? So many of us are still so impressed, and I thought you could tell us some things that people don't realize about it.
WALT: Well, *Fantasia* was made at a time when we had that feeling that we had to open the doors here—this medium was something we felt a responsibility for, and we just felt that we could go beyond the comic strip, that we could do some very exciting entertaining and beautiful things with music and picture and color and things, and so we just went ahead and tried it out and as I see it, it was successful for what it was. Of course, it brought in the art side, it brought in the music side, it brought in the motion picture, and we had all of these people who were acting as reviewers or critics. And you just can't please everybody. I learned a long time ago. I don't pay attention to these so-called critics. The real critic is that great American public out there. The world public.

If they don't like it, and they don't come then that's an answer. But if they like it I don't care what these so-called critics or reviewers say, because they're only one guy on a paper, or one guy in a magazine. To me, they've lost touch. They're living in a different world than I live in.

FOWLER: You don't ask for praise, you don't have to take critism, is that right, sir?

WALT: I feel I'm making pictures for the great public and not for a certain select few. Now that was true with *Fantasia* in that those purists in the musical world, they frowned on this. They even—some of the critics said, "Why does Disney have to put pictures to music, can't we sit and listen to music and make our own pictures?"

But there is a great segment of that audience, that by seeing the pictures to *Fantasia* became acquainted with some of this classical music. And it even led to them becoming interested in other classics that were not represented in *Fantasia*. And I think *Fantasia* made a real contribution to opening a door there for an awful lot of people . . . in getting them excited—young children, when they play the records and see the music, they begin to appreciate music. So I think we made a contribution, but you can never please the purists.

That's true with my nature films. I've had some of these so-called purists in the world of nature criticize me. They say, "Disney personalizes these little animals." That's the way I see little animals, I can't help it. I see a little rabbit, or I watch them, or I follow a cat or a dog. I personalize them. It's an intuitive thing with me. But you just can't please everybody, and I don't want to please everybody. Because I'd be a little worried if I did something and everybody was pleased with it. In fact, when one of these critics praise one of my pictures back there, I really get worried. If I'm pleasing *them*, maybe I won't please that great big audience that I love out there.

FOWLER: In spite of the egghead fringe of criticism, you have received many accolades from many columnists for many years. And does this kind of appreciation give you energy and make it easier to work?

WALT: Well, yes. You're always happy when somebody recognizes something in the things you do as deserving of a mention that way. It's a wonderful thing to have the feeling that different nations around the world that have honored us and have sort of taken us in. There are many awards that nobody's ever heard about and that is in some of the countries they classify our films as being beyond the commercial, as being cultural, and we're allowed to come in without certain taxes that are put on other films . . . duties.

And to be well-received in these countries is something to be grateful for. But again, most of these awards and things have come from the people . . . they are represented by how we've pleased the people in a country, where the government sees fit to honor us. I don't know if I ever got one from the critic's circle or not in New York. The Academy of course is voted on by the great membership in the Academy.

FOWLER: What do you think of *Look*'s critic, Gary Zimmerman? Did he do a good job in the space you had in facing the development of the Disney studios?
WALT: That's the first time I knew that Zimmerman was a critic.

FOWLER: Well, he's not a critic—he's an article man.
WALT: It's a good thing I didn't know when I was talking to him. (laughter)

FOWLER: Well, he enjoyed his work, and wanted you to enjoy it too.
WALT: That's right . . . I read that this morning.

FOWLER: It's almost impossible to read in that photostat.
WALT: That's so. I have one criticism of it though . . .

FOWLER: What's that?
WALT: It wasn't long enough. (laughter) It didn't give us enough pages.

FOWLER: There's five. Well, it looks bigger in color. You have to think I'm crazy for asking this and if you answer it, there's some danger that some people might thing you are . . . but, Mickey Mouse has been pretty close to Walt Disney for a long time. You were speaking of seeing little animals as you see an otter at play and you think of children at a fairground or something. What's the closest you have ever come to thinking about Mickey as really being a creature, not a cartoon? Did you ever have an experience like this?
WALT: Back in those days, when I was making nothing but the Mickey comics, yes, I always thought of him as a personality. There were things that he would do and there were things that he just couldn't do. I would think of it this way, "Now this is something that Mickey could do." So we always thought of him as a personality. But it reached a point . . . I never thought of him as a mouse . . . we thought of him more as a little

boy. And that's how Pluto came to be and it was kind of incongruous that a mouse could have a dog as big as Pluto. But we kind of forgot the fact that he was a mouse.

Early in the Mickey Mouse series he started out as a little boy in effect, in a barnyard with all the other animals, and Lindbergh had just crossed the Atlantic. So he was building his own airplane in the barnyard. And that was the first Mickey Mouse.

Now, later on, I got back and had him as a mouse, and it wasn't well received. The distributor wrote to me and said, "You've done something to Mickey, we've lost him." And it's because we brought him down, and we thought of him as a mouse. Then I went back and thought of him as I originally did, and he went on from there. He was a little fellow, is what he actually was, a little fellow . . . a mouse about as small as you can get.

Of course, the heavy was always this big cat, more like a human cat, but I always thought of Mickey as a little fellow. And Mickey had to have certain types of situations and things . . . he was only good for certain things. I compared him to Harold Lloyd. Mickey in himself wasn't funny, he was cute. So the situation had to make Mickey funny. Now when the duck came along, the duck was just the opposite, and he was created to give us another character, an opposite personality. He was comic within himself. He supplied something that we just couldn't do with Mickey. It was what I called a situation comic, and the duck was the comic.

FOWLER: One more thing . . . from art to business, you don't seem to have any hangups about contributing in both areas . . . were you flattered that five major American industries asked *you* to be in charge of their representation in their exhibit at the New York World's Fair?
WALT: Yes, we were, and that was a direct result of our building of Disneyland where we went into another dimension in what we call "three-dimension" type of shows. It has lead to this thing, and after the World's Fair we've taken a step beyond anything we have at Disneyland. Of course, everything that we're doing for the fair, for these concerns, we hope will eventually have their permanent home at Disneyland. That was part of it. And if that thought hadn't been in mind, we wouldn't have gotten into this World's Fair thing at all. But it's only two years, that fair, and when it's over with we hope that every one of the exhibits there can be brought back to Disneyland. The big thing to me is Disneyland. I've started it . . . not only keep it going . . . but keep it building to a

point that it can never be topped. How many more millions that'll take, I don't know. There's always a problem of keeping a things up to date. It's like your automobile . . . ten years later, there are improvements you can put in to make it more efficient, to make it much better . . . and that's what we're doing with Disneyland.

We re-engineer things, completely change them, because we've found a better way to do it. That all helps make the park more interesting but also in the way of maintenance, upkeep and operational costs which we have to keep pace with. Because like any other business, that scale is rising. Our wage scale is going up every year, you know? So you wonder how can you keep pace? So we have to keep re-engineering and rebuilding some of these things. Finding better ways to make it operate more efficiently and make it more fun for the public. So it's like changing car models every so often . . . you have to do it.

FOWLER: . . . new opportunities or innovations for motion pictures and television, has everything been done, or is it a big, wide open field?
WALT: Well, movies reached a point here where they couldn't quite understand why people weren't coming to the theaters the way they had, and there was a certain panic that set in, so they went for bigger screens and Cinemascope and Cinerama and those things. They did put on certain shows that did attract people, but at the time I kept feeling that those things were wonderful, and I used them myself. We have the 360° screen, but I use it for shows like Disneyland. But as far as the movies went, it still comes down to a good story that has an appeal to a broader audience. That big audience is still out there. But you've got to have the film that appeals to them. They're more selective now. So at the very time they were bringing out the wide screens, I even brought one to the theaters that was very successful that had been shot on 16 mm film. Then they said everything had to have color. And during this whole binge that they were on, I made one called *The Shaggy Dog* that was black & white. And it was a very, very successful motion picture. And it proved my point . . . that regardless of these innovations—wider screens and all of that—and I've gone for all of them myself—I was the first to bring stereophonic sound and I still believe in it—in *Fantasia* in 1940.

At that time with *Fantasia* I wanted to put a wider screen. I wanted to double my screen and I was all set to do it, but the bankers had their foot on my neck and I had to go along with the conventional. But I still had my stereophonic sound. So I believe in those things but still all these things can only go so far. The novelty wears off quick and if you don't have a good story, if it isn't well produced and it isn't made for what I call the movie audience—the movie audience is a big audience. And, of course, you can make movies for that small segment like those who love the foreign movies . . . and you can make all those movies you want to. But I think the responsibility of anybody running a studio like we do is to make movies not for that certain 10 percent, but to make it for the masses. That's what I do and I love to do that.

80 Million a Year from Fantasy

FRANK RASKY / 1964

From *Star Weekly* (Toronto), November 14, 1964, pp. 8–11. Reprinted courtesy of *The Toronto Star Syndicate*.

Walt Disney's ears perked up, mouselike. I had just informed him he had once won a gold medal for me.

"Oh?" he inquired, all attention. "How did that happen?"

I told him it happened twenty years back at Oakwood Collegiate in Toronto. "I entered the school oratory contest," I said, "and my speech was all about you and Mickey Mouse. I can still remember my closing line."

"Tell me. What was it?"

"It was kind of corny," I said, "but I really meant it. My eulogy ended, 'And so, Walt Disney labored like a mountain—and produced a mouse!' It won first prize. I've waited all these years to thank you and Mickey."

Disney picked up a gold statue from his desk and his stubby, square-cut fingers fondly caressed it. "I've got twenty-nine of these Academy Awards," he said. "But this Oscar I treasure most of all. It was my first prize. Mickey won it for me back in 1932."

He gazed out of the office window and his eyes swept across his fifty-acre Walt Disney Studios outside. "My little cartoon factory," he persists in calling it, though it now grosses $80 million a year and it has long since spilled over into 350 businesses that embrace far more than cartoons. The capital of an enchanted empire that has turned out 575 motion pictures, it now produces feature-length films and nature films, television shows and amusement-park shows; it publishes song sheets and records, books and magazines; it syndicates comic strips in one thousand newspapers; and it collects royalties for a myriad of Disney products, ranging from Snow White dolls to Donald Duck toidy seats, from seven hundred manufacturers in forty nations around the world.

Disney's eyes dollied back to the statuette in his hands. "It all began with Mickey," he said. "And I'm duly grateful to him. You know, he's no longer a young pipsqueak. Neither am I. I was twenty-seven when I first impersonated him. I tried to speak in a child's falsetto instead of my flat mid-western twang. Nowadays when we rerun the Mouse cartoons on TV, we have to speed them up to put his voice into higher register."

Disney set down the statuette. He lit up one of the French Gitanes cigarettes that he tensely chainsmokes. "Imagine it," he said in a sad voice. "Mickey is thirty-six now. I guess the Mouse and I have both let old age sneak up on us."

At sixty-two, Disney is far from being elderly in spirit. But it's true he does look remarkably like a middle-aged version of the mouse who led the vanguard of little Disney animals that have crept hippety-hopping, into the heart of humankind. Disney has a pointed face, big ears, gray-ing moustache, a long, sensitive nose. What distinguishes him most markedly from his premier cartoon creation are his brown eyes. To be sure, they can at times be sharp, animated and buttonlike in Mickey Mouse fashion. But most of the time they appear hooded, glassy and mournful, as though they were focusing on some brighter, happier Never Never Land of long ago when he was a boy.

I had called on Disney because I wanted to see how the mind of a genius works. In Hollywood, of course, the word "genius" is tossed around as promiscuously as "darling." But it has always seemed to me that Disney and Charlie Chaplin are the only two authentic geniuses that Hollywood ever spawned.

I asked Disney whether he had ever known Chaplin.

"Yes, Charlie was very kind to me," he said. "When everybody else was sceptical, he encouraged me to go ahead with my first feature-length animated film. Even let my bookkeepers examine all his books so I could lick the problems of distribution. 'Don't let the cynics or the bankers sell you short on *Snow White*,' Charlie told me. 'It'll be your biggest success.' "

Chaplin was an accurate forecaster, for *Snow White* proved to be one of the ten all-time top grossers in the motion-picture industry. Yet Disney remembers Chaplin as more than an astute businessman.

"I learned a lot about storytelling from Charlie," Disney said. "He was full of fun. Loved to clown and act out his stories. I was with him once at Santa Anita racetrack. He was demonstrating to me the sight gags for his next picture. 'Now the Little Fellow does this,' he pantomimed. 'Then he does that.' Charlie got so engrossed in his recital he didn't notice the crowds gathering around us. And the crowds got so wrapped up in the pathos of his characterization that they forgot all about the race."

Disney chuckled at the memory, and he went on, "Charlie taught me that in the best comedy you've got to feel sorry for your main character. Before you laugh with him, you've got to shed a tear for him. That was the trouble with our *Alice in Wonderland*. Lewis Carroll's Alice wasn't a sympathetic character. She was a prim, prissy girl who bumped into a lot of weird nonsense figures. We fell down in *Alice* because we were trying to please Carroll's specialized egghead public as well as the mass public. Well, I learned you can't please both."

"Is that why you lost money on *Fantasia*, too?" I asked.

On the contrary, Disney felt that two other things contributed to its immediate failure at the box-office. When he released *Fantasia* in 1939, Europe was in a war-jittery state; and that market was too unsettled to accept musical fantasy. Furthermore, his bankers were too impatient to recoup their $2,200,000 investment in *Fantasia*; they wouldn't let Disney release it the way he wanted—as a widescreen, three-dimensional-sound film, showcased in deluxe theatres on a reserved-seat basis.

"I guess I was fifteen years ahead of my time," Disney says. "Because when I re-released *Fantasia* in the 1950s in its original form, it more than recouped its losses."

Not that Disney claims *Fantasia* is a masterpiece of art. "The truth is I can't stand to look at *Fantasia* today," he said. "Just as I can't tolerate *Snow White*. I was pressured into releasing both pictures for the Christmas trade before I was fully satisfied with them. I think Snow White's nose is too wiggly. And even though I have a tin ear musically, I recognize that some of the *Fantasia* whimsy is overly cute."

Snow White and the Seven Dwarfs, © Disney Enterprises, Inc.

I reminded Disney of the criticism made by intellectuals—that all his cartoons were cutely sentimentalized, picture-postcard art—and I asked him what he thought of abstract artists.

"I may be a sentimentalist," Disney said, "but if so, millions of sentimentalists have taste as schmaltzy as mine. As for abstract painters, some are bad craftsmen—frauds pretending to be artists. Picasso tantalizes while he puzzles me. I never know if he's a fine draftsman consciously avoiding exact images, or a brilliant doodler simply enjoying himself."

I asked Disney whether another criticism of the intelligentsia bothered him—that he was a one-man league of decency, whose films were all resolutely wholesome, and that he was squeamish about mention of that

ugly word, s-e-x. "Does this mean you are intentionally a prude?"
I inquired.

"That's like asking whether I've stopped beating my wife," Disney
said. "Certainly I believe sex—the love a boy has for a girl—is natural.
But I believe there are other kinds of love as well. There's the love a
mother has for a child, as in *Bambi*, or a child for a dog, as in *Old Yeller*.
What I look for are stories with a universal appeal. An American stand-
up comedian is apt to flop in Japan, say, because his jokes are too local-
ized. But my *Parent Trap* was a smashing success in Japan, because the
whole world understands the humor that arises from family life."

By now, Disney is convinced that certain classical themes—man or
beast pitted against nature—automatically ought to be stamped with the
Disney imprimatur. He cited the case of *The Incredible Journey*. This was
the story about two dogs and a cat who travel across Canada, written by
the Port Arthur, Ontario, author, Sheila Burnford. When Disney and a
second producer bid for the film rights, Miss Burnford set a high price
on her novel. Both producers agreed to meet that price, and so Miss
Burnford had to decide between them.

"Naturally, she chose us," Disney said. "It would have been wrong
for anyone else to do her animal story. I later found out the other
bidding producer was George Seaton. 'Sorry I didn't let it go for a
cheaper price, Walt,' he told me. 'I should've *known* it was a
Disney picture.' "

Disney may also have been swayed to make *The Incredible Journey*
because he concedes he has a soft spot in his heart for Canada. His
father, Elias Disney, was a Canadian, born on a farm at Bluevale, Ontario
near Goderich. "I've visited the Bluevale pioneer cemetery where my
French-Irish grandparents were buried," Disney says. "I write often to
my Canadian cousins living up there—the Richardsons and Pearsons.
A Richardson keeps up the old log cabin where my grandmother
and granddad were married. As for the Pearsons, I believe I'm related
to Prime Minister Lester Pearson on my grandmother's side of the
family."

Walt Disney, however, was born in Chicago and brought up in Kansas
City. His boyhood was no rosy Peter Pan fairytale; and it may be that he
later took to the make-believe world to escape from his harsh environment. His father was a strict disciplinarian, who whipped him until he
was fourteen. When he was ten, the boy was forced to get up at 3:30
each morning to deliver the Kansas City Star in order to support his

impoverished family. Disney still suffers nightmares in which he dreams he has missed a customer along his newspaper route. He wakes up sweating and thinking, "I'll have to rush back and leave a paper before Dad finds out."

He remembers as idyllic the few times he paused on verandas of rich homes along his paper route to play with borrowed toys. "I'll never forget how one of those kids evidently had a party the night before," he recalls. "I sat there in the early dawn eating a box of candy and racing an electric train left behind. It was fifteen minutes of stolen delight and I've never been able to recapture that moment of enchantment."

Later, while eking out a meagre living as illustrator for a Kansas City ad agency, Disney was inspired by office mice. "They used to fight for crumbs in my tin waste-basket when I worked alone late at night," he says. "I lifted them out and kept them in wire cages on my desk. I grew particularly fond of one brown house mouse. He was a timid little guy. By tapping him on the nose with my pencil, I trained him to run inside a black circle I drew on my drawing board. When I left Kansas to try my luck in Hollywood, I hated to leave him behind. So I carefully carried him to a backyard, making sure it was a nice neighborhood, and the tame little fellow scampered to freedom."

This pet brown mouse, of course, was the model for the incomparable Mickey. Legendary is the story of how Disney was riding in a train with his wife, Lillian, in the summer of 1928 when he dreamed up the idea of making animated cartoons to star Mortimer Mouse. His wife, Disney's former secretary, thought that Mortimer sounded too sissified, and thus the equally alliterative Mickey Mouse was born.

Though his wife's opinion proved valid in that case, Disney has not solicited her critical judgment ever since she raised femininely heated objections to his making of *Snow White*. "But, honey, I've got our mortgage sunk into this movie," he remembers pleading with her. "What have you got against the Snow White story?"

"I can't stand the sight of dwarfs!" she retorted. "I predict nobody'll ever pay a dime to see a dwarf picture."

With his first $3 million profits from *Snow White*, Disney built his studio in Burbank. He expresses wide-eyed wonderment at the way it has since grown, transforming him into a sort of modern Merlin ruling over a global assembly line. "Just the other day," he says, "my brother, Roy, told me, 'Do you know that our payroll for one week is $750,000?' I couldn't believe it."

Of the manifold projects currently occupying his magical wand—and his staff of 2,200 unionized elves—Disney was most eager to talk about these goodies:

- On the drawing boards now are two feature-length animated extravaganzas, A. A. Milne's *Winnie the Pooh* (to be released next year) and Rudyard Kipling's *Jungle Book* (possibly for Christmas in 1966). Disney's live-action spectacular this Christmas will be *Mary Poppins*. This is a two-hour and twenty minute musical version of the P. L. Travers children's classic about an English nursemaid who flies through the air holding her umbrella. (Disney revealed to me how its star, Julie Andrews, shown air-borne on our *Star Weekly* cover, manages this trick. Strung under her arms beneath her clothes is a corset-like harness, which is attached to thin piano wire. The wire is darkened with shoe polish, so it won't reflect light, and special camera angles render the wire invisible to the eye. The wire is linked to pulleys that move on wheels on a track out of camera sight, and a technician with a crane steers her on her flight ten feet up in the air.)
- His forthcoming nature films will deal with wild life in Arizona and the coyotes of North America; a third about eagles and a fourth about wolverines. ("I've got camera units prowling all over the darn place," Disney says.)
- To join his prize-winning educational films, *Donald Duck in Mathemagic Land* and *Donald Duck and the Wheel*, Disney is putting the finishing touches on *Money, Money, Money*, a history of currency starring Donald's uncle, Scrooge McDuck. ("Don't call the things 'educational,'" Disney says. "That word's poison to kids. Nobody wants to be educated. They want to be entertained while they're being informed.")
- For his weekly one-hour NBC show, *Walt Disney's Wonderful World of Color*, he has dispatched Toronto TV director Norman Campbell to Copenhagen to shoot a Disney epic about the Royal Copenhagen Ballet. ("Your CBC is the best film training ground in the world today," Disney said. "Another of your Toronto graduates, Arthur Hiller, did a masterly job of directing our picture, *Miracle of the White Stallions*.")
- Canadian impresarios have consulted with him to see if Disney can come up with wizardry for the Montreal World's Fair of 1967 that will surpass the seemingly miraculous talking robots he devised for the present New York World's Fair. ("I disagreed with the Montreal showmen about their scheme to separate their exhibits by several

miles," he told me. "This is the age of wheels, and people don't like doing that much walking. For that matter, I'm really opposed to all World's Fairs. They last only two seasons, then are torn down.")

Disney reserves his most enraptured planning for Disneyland, his $45 million-investment, sixty-five-acre private dream world at Anaheim, California, which he shares with 5,500,000 yearly visitors from around the world. He so delights in the place that he maintains a secret apartment over its fire-house on Main Street; from this secluded vantage point, he can watch the kiddies enjoying themselves on Saturday afternoons.

Disney rolled out a big blueprint chart in his office, and his eyes glowed with boyish excitement as he outlined to me his plan for a New Orleans haunted house that he wants to add to Disneyland next year. The cartoon king's voice grew high-pitched and spooky as he assumed the guise of the "ghost host" who would welcome about eighty guests crowded into the mansion's scary elevator.

"The doors of the panelled elevator close," Disney explained. "Then the people inside can't see a thing. All they can hear is the voice of the ghost host wailing, friendly like, 'Folks, don't let your imagination get the better of you.' Gradually the frightened people notice that the elevator elongates by thirty feet. The pictures on the side of the elevator elongate. The panels elongate. The whole goldarn thing elongates. 'By the way, folks', the ghost cackles, 'you better hold hands with each other, because the doors have vanished. Ho! Ho! Ho! Remember, you paid to get in. Do you know how to get out? You should have thought of that before. Woo! Woo! Woo! Who ever heard of doors in a haunted house?' "

Disney laughed, and put away his blueprint as though it were a toy. "My haunted house will be populated with a thousand and one spooks and witches and ogres, but you can bet there's one thing it won't contain," he said. "Just as in my home in Holmby Hills and my Smoketree ranch in Palm Springs, you'll not find a single mousetrap around the house. I've never forgotten it was a mouse made me what I am today."

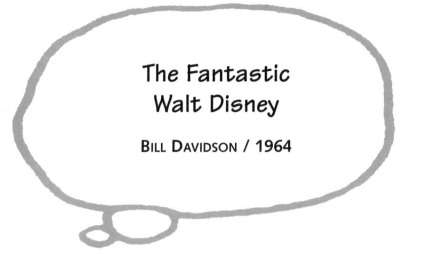

The Fantastic
Walt Disney

BILL DAVIDSON / 1964

From *Saturday Evening Post*, vol. 237,
no. 38, November 7, 1964, pp. 66–68,
71–75. Copyright © 1964 Renewed.
Used with permission of BFL & MS, Inc.

Not long ago one of the leading French magazines made a startling and
completely serious proposal: that Walt Disney be awarded the 1964
Nobel Peace Prize. At about the same time an equally startling and
equally serious movement was launched in California: to make Disney
the rapid-transit czar of Los Angeles. The sixty-two-year-old Disney, a
noted turf kicker of the Gary Cooper school, modestly disassociated
himself from both of these suggestions. A few weeks later, however,
came the most unexpected honor of them all. President Johnson awarded
Disney the Presidential Medal of Freedom, the highest decoration the
United States Government can bestow on a civilian.

All this seems to show how far you can go by being an irascible, stubborn nonconformist, completely out of step with the rest of the entertainment world. For Disney—who fits none of the molds—dominates his industry in a way that no other man does today.

In a business in which people sometimes seem obsessed with sex and brutality, Disney continues to prosper with simple little films and TV shows about precocious animals, winsome children and the heroes and heroines of unsophisticated Victorian literary classics. His Disneyland park, brimming with wholesome mechanical wonders, continues to outdraw all the girlie shows and tunnels of love in nearly all the other amusement parks in the United States combined. His four exhibits at the New York World's Fair (featuring dancing dolls, homespun Americana and a Fantasia-like view of Creation and prehistoric life) drew an average of about 135,000 people per day through the first season—or about ten times the number who went to see the chorus cuties who were a flop in the fair's amusement area.

It is difficult to live anywhere in the civilized world today without being within range of at least one Walt Disney production. In addition to his four shows at the fair, Disney's film musical, *Mary Poppins* (at $5,175,000, the most expensive movie he has ever made), currently is playing at the Radio City Music Hall in New York. The movie critics almost unanimously have called it one of the finest films of the year. At the same time no fewer than six other Disney pictures are in release in the U.S. and elsewhere—*The Sword in the Stone*, *The Incredible Journey*, *The Misadventures of Merlin Jones*, *A Tiger Walks*, *The Three Lives of Thomasina* and *The Moon-Spinners*—and his regular Sunday-evening television series on NBC has just been renewed for another two years. *Pinocchio* and *Snow White* and old Mickey Mouse short subjects keep playing unendingly in U.S. theaters and in countries like Pakistan and Nigeria, and Disney TV reruns fill the airwaves in Europe, Africa and Asia.

At present, Disney has two full-length feature cartoons in preparation, as well as three live-action movies and twenty-five new one-hour shows for his TV series. But that's not all. Disney also is adding a five-million-dollar New Orleans Square to Disneyland, along with a haunted mansion filled with ghosts, hobgoblins and assorted fiends. He is about to help rehabilitate the St. Louis waterfront with a new multimillion-dollar Disneyland-type establishment under a three-acre roof. He is considering a proposal to erect an amphitheater at Niagara Falls, in which he will dramatize the spectacle of the falls at all four seasons of the year. And he has staggering plans under way for a huge amusement park in Japan, to re-create the various periods of that country's history. These future holdings will be added to the already vast complex of Disney entertainment projects that grossed nearly $82 million in the last fiscal year.

It is now thirty-seven years since Disney first introduced Mickey Mouse—and himself—to the world with the classic cartoon short, *Steamboat Willie*, and his admirers in Hollywood and elsewhere have been puzzling ever since over the reasons for his persistent and spectacular success. He violates all the rules for Hollywood behavior. When Darryl Zanuck or Jack Warner or any other studio head visits a movie location, the preparations for the arrival of the Presence resemble those for a state visit, with limousines, a vice-presidential honor guard, etc.; Disney shows up unannounced in the cheapest possible rented car which he has picked up at the nearest airport. Other executives maintain a corps of lackeys to tailor and refresh their clothes, to cut their hair, and even to answer the phones in their Rolls-Royces; Disney presides over his operations unattended, in rumpled store-bought suits and with unshorn hair.

In an era in which the control of movie studios is passing more and more into the hands of committees, banks, boards of directors and other outsiders, Disney's reign over his empire remains as autocratic and absolute as was that of Louis B. Mayer during the heyday of M-G-M. Nobody buys or sells or creates *anything* at the Walt Disney studios without the OK and involvement of the big man himself. Although everyone at the studio, from janitor to associate producer, calls him "Walt," the "Walt" is spoken in tones of deference. Not long ago a well-known executive came over from another film company to work as an associate on a Walt Disney production. The first day on the job the executive was annoyed by the sound of a lawn mower outside his window, and he shouted at the gardener to desist. An hour later the executive received a call from Disney's secretary, informing him that Disney wanted to see him. The executive rushed over and Disney said, "You spoke harshly to that man. He's been with me for twenty years. I don't want it to happen again." The executive mumbled a contrite, "Yes, sir." Disney continued, "And there's another thing I want you to remember. There's only one s.o.b. at this studio—and that's me."

While most Hollywood studios abound with stories of the extracurricular love lives of their executives and stars, no scandal has ever touched the Disney lot. Walt himself has been the most devoted of husbands (he married one of his assistants, Lillian Bounds, thirty-nine years ago, and they have two daughters and six grandchildren). Most Hollywood studios cram as much realistic sex into their pictures as the censors will allow, but in a Disney production, romance has barely developed beyond the stage where Tom Mix would chastely and almost simultaneously kiss the heroine and his horse, Tony. The only time Disney ever allowed a racy incident to creep into one of his films was in *Bon Voyage*, when Fred MacMurray unwittingly became involved with a French prostitute. "It was a disaster," says Disney, mopping his brow at the recollection. "The fourteen-year-olds in my audience didn't understand the scene— and I guess *I* didn't understand it, either." William H. Anderson, Disney's vice president in charge of studio operations, says, "I guess Walt is the only man in Hollywood to whom you don't tell a dirty joke. When you do, somehow it doesn't come out funny."

For all his outward simplicity, however, Disney actually is an extremely complicated man. One critic described him as having nineteenth-century emotions in conflict with a twenty-first-century brain." His prissiness sometimes seems to be studied—like the smiling, grandfatherly face he presents to the TV camera—as part of a shrewd campaign to retain his hold on the so-called "family audience." There's a somewhat calculated air, too, about the homespun stories he tells, such as the one about how "Pa was of the generation that didn't believe in borrowing money, and he offered to help me out with two hundred dollars when I was eight *million* dollars in the hole trying to build my studio."

Disney thinks nothing of flitting from project to project in his company's private jet, but he wastes a lot of his time checking burned-out electric-light bulbs and dirty washrooms. He'll spend millions on electronic innovations, but he's known as Hollywood's most tight-fisted man with a dollar when it comes to dealing with actors, writers and employees. The history of his studio has been marked with long and bitter labor strife over unionization and wage demands. Practically all of his competitors in the cartoon field are former Disney men who left the fold because of some such dispute. His fees to actors and writers are much lower than the industry average, and his contracts for the purchase of books from authors are unique in Hollywood. Not only does Disney sew up a book (usually at cut-rate prices) for every possible use, including games, comics and puzzles based on the author's characters, but a letter accompanies the contract with waivers to be signed "by the author's wife and each of his children" so that not even the writer's death can thwart Disney's continuing control over the material.

Disney's inconsistency has drawn the fire of critics in that he constantly crusades against theaters running horror films and sadistic melodramas on the same bill with his pictures, and yet plenty of horror and sadism creeps into his own movies. A leopard killing an antelope calf in *The African Lion*, Mickey Mouse belting an adversary with a sledgehammer, Goofy being tripped so that he crashes into a wall, are examples that have been cited. Indeed, the witch in *Snow White* probably has caused more children's nightmares than Frankenstein's monster and Godzilla combined. Disney admits receiving hundreds of letters to this effect from irate parents, but he has a simple answer. He says, "I showed *Snow White* to my own two daughters when they were small, and when they came to me later and said they wanted to play witch, I figured it was all right to let other kids see the witch."

Disney has been criticized, too, for gathering a tremendous number of talented people into his organization, making use of their creativity, and then putting the whole thing out under the fanfare, "Walt Disney presents. . . ." He used to be an artist, but he doesn't draw anymore. Neither does he write. He explains, however: "I'm like a bee that flits from flower to flower, taking a little pollen here, a little pollen there, and I build up the honey in the honeycomb."

As unfeeling as this sometimes is to the flowers that make the pollen, it is one of the reasons Disney is considered an authentic genius of our time. He is a human catalyst, a man with a miraculously compartmented mind, who can go to a meeting about Disneyland, then to a meeting about a television show, then to a meeting about a movie—and in each instance remember what was said by the same people a month before, sop up their newest information, and then move on.

As the late Jerry Wald once said, "Like Thomas Alva Edison, Disney has eyes that see what no other man sees." He can look at a bird's awkward mating dance and choreograph it into a comic ballet in one of his nature films; he can stare at a doorknob and, by adding a mouth here and ears there, can convert it into one of the most engaging characters in his cartoon feature, *Alice in Wonderland*. He is, in effect, a modern-day wizard, imparting human characteristics—which he alone sees—to mice, owls, otters, seals, crickets, to sugar bowls and a host of other inanimate objects, transmuting commonplace materials into artistic gold.

Charles Levy, a Disney executive who has been with him for many years, has a theory of his own about Disney's talent. Levy says, "Walt restlessly prowls the earth like a walking electronic computer storing up data. You never know when he's going to press a button, and some idea, maybe from as far back as 1910, will come tumbling out of his brain." All of Disney's World's Fair exhibits, for example, are applications of the new science of audio-animatronics, in which amazingly lifelike plastic figures move, walk, speak or roar (according to the species) with uncanny fidelity to the real models. Signals are fed from electronic tape to a transistorized "brain" in the figure, which, in turn, activates little motors that operate legs, arms, lips, etc. Sound, too, is fed from the tape to coincide with the lip movements. Thus, when Disney's Abraham Lincoln rises from his chair in the Illinois Pavilion and makes a speech on patriotism to the audience, he winks, blinks and frowns, and is almost indistinguishable from a live actor.

"And yet," says Levy, "this is an idea that has been stored away in Walt's brain since 1945. I remember seeing him at the studio then, and he was all wrapped up in something mysterious he was doing with Buddy Ebsen, who, in those days, was a fine dancer. He had Buddy do a dance number, and there were men in the room punching holes in what seemed to be a mechanical piano roll. Then I saw Walt playing with little Buddy Ebsen dolls, which were attached by electric wires to a huge console-type machine. The men would feed the piano rolls into the console like a continuous I.B.M. card, and the little Buddy Ebsen dolls would repeat the dance steps I had seen Ebsen himself do. It didn't work because those were the days before transistors and the equipment was too cumbersome, so Walt put the whole thing aside. But now it's nineteen years later, and I go to the World's Fair and I see Walt's Lincoln and fighting dinosaurs and dancing children. It's been refined by electronics but it's the Buddy Ebsen idea all over again. He carried it around with him all those years until finally he was able to make it work."

Similarly, Disney recalls that years ago, when he first read A. A. Milne's classic, *Winnie-the-Pooh*, he came to the part where Winnie, a bear, got his rear end stuck in a rabbit hole. Young Walt, then fifteen, spent hours wondering about something that isn't in the book: What was it like for the rabbit suddenly to have a bear's rear end as a more or less permanent part of the decor of his home? Forty-seven years later, exactly such a scene has been added to Disney's feature cartoon version of *Winnie-the-Pooh*, which is now in production. As Disney explains it,

"The rabbit tries to disguise the rear end with a moose head. Then he puts it in a picture frame with a rural scene painted on it. Eventually, he drapes a sheet around it and it looks like a chair. I think it might be my funniest scene in the picture."

As for Disney's fierce drive, it probably stems from recurrent bouts with adversity from his earliest to his middle years. Disney's father, Elias, a French-Irish-Canadian, and his mother, Flora, a German-American, had an uncommonly difficult time raising their family, first going bankrupt trying to grow oranges in Florida and later struggling along with a carpenter shop in Chicago, where Walt was born on December 5, 1901. "My mother," Walt says, "used to go out on a construction job and hammer and saw planks with the men." When the carpentry business failed, Disney's father made a stab at running a meager little farm in Marceline, Missouri. Young Walt was the fourth of five children. He has one younger sister and three older brothers, two of whom couldn't take the hard life on the farm and ran off to make their own way. They ended up as a post-office clerk and an insurance salesman, respectively. One of Walt's older brothers, Roy, remained behind and the two have been inseparable ever since. Roy, now is president and general finance wizard of all the Disney enterprises.

When young Walt couldn't make enough money to support himself as a newspaper delivery boy in Kansas City, Missouri (where his family moved when he was nine), he became a candy butcher on a Kansas City-to-Chicago train. At the age of sixteen he tried to join both the Army and the Navy during World War I, was rebuffed because of his age, and then went overseas as a Red Cross ambulance driver. When he returned, an eighteen-year-old, he found high-school work boring, switched to Chicago's Academy of Fine Arts at night and tried to become an artist. Unable to make a living as an artist and cartoonist for Kansas City advertising agencies, he moved to California with $40 in his pocket to try to crack the brand-new field of movie cartoons. He got a job drawing a cartoon called *Alice in Cartoonland*, took his $2,500 fee and set up his own company with his brother Roy. He created and sold a new movie cartoon character named Oswald the Rabbit. When Disney's New York distributors claimed Oswald for their own and assigned other artists to draw him, Walt and his charming young wife Lillian thought of a tame mouse that used to poke around Walt's drawing board in Kansas City. They hocked everything, and Mickey Mouse was born.

Even during the fantastically successful years which followed the advent of Mickey, Disney had periods of adversity from which he always recovered more strongly than ever. He nearly went broke making his first full-length feature, *Snow White*, in 1937, but his $1.5 million investment has returned more than $20 million to him over the years. Just before World War II he refused to recognize a union formed by his employees, and a long, bitter strike at his studio nearly put him out of business again. But once more he recouped with his profits from *Pinocchio* and *Fantasia*. As recently as 1955 he had to borrow on his insurance to open Disneyland. Out of all the setbacks, however, came a whole world of fantasy which has permanently added to the culture of the world— Mickey Mouse, Donald Duck, Goofy, Dopey, Bambi, Jiminy Cricket, Jose Carioca, et al. They pop up in educational films, as emblems on atomic submarines and supersonic bombers, and even in such remote places as the Royal Palace of Thailand, whose King Bhumiphol is one of the world's most enthusiastic collectors of Disneyana. There also is a cast of live actors and actresses discovered or rediscovered by Disney—Hayley Mills, James Mason, Fred MacMurray, Annette Funicello, Tommy Kirk, Maureen O'Hara, Jane Wyman and Pola Negri, among others.

Perhaps his greatest casting feat is his latest. Julie Andrews had starred in *My Fair Lady* and *Camelot* on Broadway, but one studio after another had turned her down because her strong-jawed, freshly scrubbed face conflicted with the conventional idea of what a movie star was supposed to look like. The moment Disney acquired the Mary Poppins books, he rushed to New York, visited backstage at *Camelot* and asked Miss Andrews to sign for the title role. He had to wait for her to have a baby, but once the movie was made, every other studio wanted her. By casting her in *Mary Poppins*, Disney made both himself and Miss Andrews front-runners for 1964 Academy Awards.

Haunted by a rabbit

The struggle ended some time ago for Disney, but, say the associates who know him, Walt continues to act as if the struggle were still there. A Disney executive explains it this way: "Everything Walt does today is conditioned by his past problems. When he makes one of his tough deals, he negotiates like he's afraid someone might take another *Oswald the Rabbit* away from him."

Disney, unlike his smiling TV personality, is a moody, introspective man who arrives at his studio at about 8:30 every morning and reads

himself to sleep with scripts every night. His only title now is executive
producer. He gave up the offices of president, and chairman of the board
of Walt Disney Productions, saying, "I wasted too much time signing
papers," but this has not lessened his work load. Even on the days when
he does not have his usual quota of meetings, he indulges in what he
calls "prowling." This means that at any given moment a sign painter, a
gardener, an artist, a writer, might have Disney's lugubrious face, with
the strange expressionless eyes, peering over his shoulder.

Disney has practically no social life, and he rarely shows up at the
standard Hollywood functions. He and his wife, Lillian, live in a comfortable five-bedroom home in the exclusive Holmby Hills section of
Los Angeles, overlooking the towers of U.C.L.A. They weekend at
their 1,000-acre Smoke Tree Ranch in the desert near Palm Springs.
Mrs. Disney is a small, shy woman who rarely allows herself to be
photographed, even by Disney. She has devoted herself to making her
husband's home life as restful as possible. Knowing that Disney is sensitive to color, she has decorated both the Holmby Hills house and the
desert ranch retreat in the quiet pastel shades that are most soothing to
him. The city residence is furnished with the eighteenth-century antiques
he likes; at the ranch she has created an everblooming garden of multi-
colored flowers at which he sometimes stares in wonder for hours.

Lillian, in her unobtrusive way, has always helped Disney with his
work, and she without a doubt is the only person in the world who can
induce him to buy something he doesn't want to buy. Recently, Disney
grumbled, "Last year Lillian told me she had read an exciting novel
about a jewel robbery called *The Moon-Spinners* and that I ought to
make a picture out of it. I read it and told her it wouldn't work dramati-
cally, but she said, 'Yes, it would,' and I bought it. I had a devil of a time
getting a script, and finally we had to change the plot, add new characters, and so on. When the picture finally was finished, I showed it to
Lillian and she said triumphantly, 'See? It's just like the book.' "

When their daughters, Diane and Sharon, were youngsters, Disney
used to try out his new cartoon characters on them, but they weren't
impressed, he says, "until they saw one of my sex-education pictures in
school." Today he similarly uses his six grandchildren, mostly for their
reactions to proposed innovations at Disneyland. The grandchildren
provide Disney, a traditional doter, with one of his two main sources of
relaxation, and it is not unusual for him to be seen tooling along a Los
Angeles expressway in his convertible with huge cutouts of Donald Duck

or Ludwig Von Drake propped up in the back seat for personal delivery to young Jennifer or Walter Elias Disney Miller.

Disney's other form of relaxation is the ancient game of bowling on the green. He used to be an active polo player, but he gave that up. He also was quite a machine-shop hobbyist, and he built a small-scale railroad, complete with steam locomotive and tracks, around his Holmby Hills estate. "It was a lot of fun," says Disney, "but it got so that everyone else was riding around in the train, enjoying themselves, while I was wearing myself out stoking coal all day. I finally packed the thing up and shipped it off to Disneyland." He is occasionally tempted to bring the railroad back for his grandchildren, but on reflection he always decides it's easier to give them tickets for the amusement park.

There is no question that Disney's attitude toward his own family has contributed to his current status in Hollywood as the phenomenon of the age. Both his feature-length cartoons, now produced at the rate of one every two years, and his live-action features bear the same stamp of acceptability to children as well as adults. Disney makes what he calls "pictures that children are not embarrassed to take their parents to," and nobody else seems to be making them successfully.

Why? Disney says, "There's no magic to my formula. Maybe it's because I don't have to account to a lot of other guys, like bankers and boards of directors. Maybe it's because I just make what *I* like—good human stories where you can get with people and which prove that the better things of life can be as interesting as the sordid things. It's the old fairy-tale formula with the happy ending. People like to root for Cinderella and the Prince. If there *is* a secret to what I do—and where maybe my competitors make their mistake—I guess it's that I never make the pictures too childish, and so they do not become strictly children's films. I always try to get in a little satire about human foibles, like when I kidded academic pomposity in *The Absent-Minded Professor*."

And yet, as he said this, Disney's eyes darkened and he pointed to a series of identical plaques in the trophy-jammed anteroom of his office. The plaques all read, "For the Best Children's Picture." For an instant the old frustrations seemed to return as he spluttered, "They persist in giving me that blasted award every year. *I* don't make children's pictures. Why *do* they do it?"

The Wonderful World of Walt Disney

BILL BALLANTINE / 1966

From *Vista II*, Winter 1966–67,
pp. 30–32.

Mickey Mouse, the world's greatest ambassador of goodwill, is called
Mickey Maus in Germany, *Mik-kii Mat-su* in Japan, *Mikki Hiiri* in
Finland, *Topolino* in Italy, and south of our border he is *Raton Mickey*.

Walter Elias Disney, creator of this now legendary animated-cartoon
character, is known all over the globe as just plain Walt. Not even
bankers call him anything but that, although he heads an amusement
and merchandising empire that has shown a more than 1,400 percent
gain in profits over the past twelve years.

The job of running this lucrative colossus—with benevolent autocratic
control—brings Walt to the Walt Disney Productions studio every working day at 8:30 a.m. He long ago grew intolerant of the confining posts
of president and chairman of the board, and now, as executive producer-
in-charge of all production, he spends much of his time on the prowl,

acting as catalyst for all facets of the highly diversified operation. Outwardly, he is simplicity personified, but close observers regard him as an extremely complicated bundle of nineteenth-century emotions in conflict with a keen twenty-first-century intellect—a modern-day wizard with a knack for transforming the dross of simple ideas into mountains of gold. David Low, the distinguished British political cartoonist, regards him as "the most significant figure in graphic art since Leonardo."

In the motion picture industry Disney is highly respected as an outstanding innovator and experimentalist. He was a pioneer in cinema sound and color (1928 and 1932, with *Mickey Mouse* shorts); the first to make an animated, feature-length film (1937, *Snow White*); and first to use stereophonic sound (1940, *Fantasia*).

I called on Mr. Walt at the studio's Animation Building, corner of Mickey Avenue and Dopey Drive. His lavish suite of offices is like the sitting and living rooms of an elegant home (there even is a custom-built piano), except for its clutter of travel mementos, a plethora of photos of family, close friends and professional associates. There is also a prideful display of shiny gold and silver trophies, medals, plaques, scrolls, loving cups and other tributes (including thirty-one Academy Awards), selected from a collection of more than 900 presented to Disney since 1931.

As I entered the sanctum-sanctorum, Walt Disney—five feet, ten inches tall and weighing about 170 pounds—stood up from behind a broad cluttered desk.

Ballantine: Walt, just what is the "Disney Touch"?
Disney: Reporters are always analyzing our approach to entertainment, but there's no magic formula. I just make what I like—warm and human stories, and ones about historic characters and events, and about animals. If there *is* a secret, I guess it's that I never make the pictures too childish, but always try to get in a little satire of adult foibles. Also, we do everything our own way, for ourselves, with no outside interference. We stay close to the fundamentals of family entertainment and recreation, and have complete voice in the marketing.

B.B.: Where did you get your phenomenal organizational ability?
W.D.: I suppose it came from my great-grandfather on my Dad's side, who brought his family over to Canada from Ireland in the 1830's and settled in virgin wilderness—had to cut down trees, dig a well, haul rocks and all that. They had to work as a unit in order to survive. My father

was the oldest of eleven children and, when Dad was nineteen years old, the entire family moved from Canada to Kansas.

B.B.: Are your ideas inspired by self-hypnosis or anything like that?
W.D.: Hypnosis? Oh, come now, let's get down to earth. No, there are no mystic messages. I get together with my group—we've got some good people here—and we bat things around. Whatever we accomplish is due to the combined effort. The organization must be with you or you don't get it done; they just say to heck with him, let him do it himself. In my organization there is respect for every individual, and we all have a keen respect for the public.

B.B.: Do you ever go stale?
W.D.: Oh, sure. There are ups and downs all the time. You reach a point, then you slump for awhile. But around here we don't look backwards for long.

B.B.: To determine what people will like do you depend upon scientific surveys or personal intuition?
W.D.: You can't use surveys as a crutch. I rely on them only to prove myself right.

B.B.: You've been called an artist, writer, businessman, inventor, naturalist, educator—just what are you?
W.D.: I'm just very curious—got to find out what makes things tick— and I've always liked working with my hands; my father was a carpenter. I even apprenticed to my own machine shop here and learned the trade. Since my outlook and attitudes are ingrained throughout our organiza- tion, all our people have this curiosity; it keeps us moving forward, exploring, experimenting, opening new doors.

B.B.: What is the most challenging subject for animation?
W.D.: Whimsey—it's tough to put into action. And children's classics always are difficult to translate into our medium, because people have such notions about them. It's better for us to have all the latitude in the world. We flopped with *Alice In Wonderland* for that very reason; never did want to do it. It's filled with weird characters.

B.B.: But you did very well with *Mary Poppins*.
W.D.: Yes, but I didn't stick to the story. There are things in the picture that aren't in the book. The author was very upset about it until she saw how the audience loved it.

B.B.: Did the advent of sound and color mark your career's turning point?

W.D.: No, it came much earlier—in 1928, when I turned down good offers from people who wanted to go partners with me after we'd hit with *Steamboat Willie*, our third Mickey Mouse short, the first one ever with sound. I'd had my bellyful of others holding me back, saying leave well enough alone. I wanted to work without a middleman. Didn't have a dime, but salary offers of $2,500 per week went in this ear and out the other. They were thinking of the fast buck, but I wanted to build, and not be taken over by someone else, like happened with my *Oswald the Rabbit* series when the New York distributor, hoping to pressure me into a more profitable deal for himself, threatened to hire away my animators. I just said go ahead, take them, I'll form my own company and do something else. Had no idea then that I'd come up with such a winner as Mickey.

B.B.: What in your early life most influenced you?

W.D.: The home environment was important. We had discipline—you don't have to beat children to have that. Self-discipline is learned by example, and my dad believed in it strongly. We always were self-sufficient, but we had no luxuries—had to earn everything we got, which is good for a boy growing up.

B.B.: Were you a brilliant student?

W.D.: No, but I was good at arithmetic and a *champ* at spelldowns! Most of the time, though, I'd be dreaming, wandering all over the place, but I could bluff it on almost anything but grammar. And I was popular—nominated for class president, but the teacher decided my grades didn't warrant such an exalted position, so I had to settle for sergeant-at-arms.

B.B.: What sort of reading did you do back then?

W.D.: American history and biographies—and I still like those subjects best. I especially admire Lincoln, because of his background, and where he went, and how he did it all himself. I've always thought well, too, of Henry Ford. He was an advanced thinker, put this country on wheels with the tin-lizzie and set up social patterns that have lasted. He had in mind the welfare of his workers; wasn't he the one who started the five-dollar day? A big moment in my life was when I got to meet him.

B.B.: Besides your parents, whom do you best recall from your boyhood?
W.D.: My Aunt Maggie from Boston, from a silverware family—not a wealthy woman, but she had a little money. She always brought me drawing tablets and crayons. I'd draw these stupid-looking things, and she'd put them up in her room and rave over them. She was big and fat, and had two laps. Whenever I'd ask to sit on her lap she'd say, "Which one?" and laugh like anything. She had such a wonderful sense of humor; I remember how she used to tell me stories and be laughing so hard at the end that sometimes she couldn't finish them. There was one about a kid losing his pants when he meets a bear. Aunt Margaret would ask me what *I'd* do in such a situation—climb a tree or run? No matter how I'd answer she'd say, "*What*? With a bare behind?" And then how she'd laugh!

B.B.: Have you ever considered operating a circus?
W.D.: We had one once at Disneyland, but it's another kind of business entirely. I'll keep my nose to my own grindstone. I've turned down Broadway musicals, and even the Metropolitan Opera. Be fun if I had the time and if they gave me the right latitude—but what would I be trying to prove?

B.B.: Do you think that in our lifetime there will be peaceful understanding between the world's peoples?
W.D.: You have to remember that our lifetime is just a little dot in the span of time.

B.B.: What is the most precious quality a man can possess?
W.D.: Tolerance.

B.B.: Will you say something about the younger generation?
W.D.: It's being maligned by the communications media, hunting for things and giving them a spotlight they don't deserve. But I have great faith in them. Why, on our Grad Nights at Disneyland there are over 50,000 young kids—the boys in coat-and-tie, the girls all in party dresses; the park is theirs. *Beautiful!* And of them all, there are only fifty or a hundred characters that we have to take care of. To the youngsters of today, I say believe in the future, the world is getting better; there still is plenty of opportunity. Why, would you believe it, when I was a kid *I* thought it was *already* too late for me to make good at anything.

Index